JOHANNES COCHLAEUS

TETRACHORDUM MUSICES

MUSICOLOGICAL STUDIES AND DOCUMENTS

ARMEN CARAPETYAN

General Editor

TETRACHORDUM MUSICES

by

JOHANNES COCHLAEUS

MUSICOLOGICAL STUDIES AND DOCUMENTS

23

JOHANNES COCHLAEUS

TETRACHORDUM MUSICES

Introduction, Translation and Transcription
by
CLEMENT A. MILLER

AMERICAN INSTITUTE OF MUSICOLOGY
1970

TO JEAN and OUR FAMILY

CONTENTS

Tetrachordū Musices Joannis Coclei Norici. Arti-

um Magistri: Nurnberge nuper
contextū: pro iuuētutis Lau-
rentiane eruditione im
primis: Dein
ad
ceterorꝫ in
musicis Tyruncu
lorū salubriorē planio-
remqꝫ eruditionez | nūc pri-
ma sui Aeditiōe Typis calcogra
phorum exaratum. deo Auspice. in lucem ꝓdit.

Bilibaldi Pirckheimer Ad Jo. Coclitem Epigrama

Ingenium Cocles tribuit tibi docta Minerua
Deliciasqꝫ Venus/pulcher Apollo lyram
At numeros faciles varia et discrimina vocum
Mercurius pariter Thespiadumqꝫ chorus
Quid mirum supas si cunctos arte canendi
Cum faueant ceptis/numina tanta tuis

Chelidonius Musophilus ad lectorem.

Delius antistes Musarum carmen olympo
Concentu vario dulcisonoqꝫ canit
Quin pelago ludunt modulamina blanda canore
Sirenes. aer audit auesqꝫ suas
Necnon et letas numeris vocalibus odas
Orpheus Elisio personat. atqꝫ Linus
Cocles pieridum socius. iuuat arte Camenas
Pegaseumqꝫ melos percinit atqꝫ docet

Huius Tetrachordi Quattuor tractatus.

Primus	De Musices elementis	
Secundus	De Musica Gregoriana	Quorū quilibet decem
Tercius	De Octo tonis Meli	capita complectitur.
Quartus	De Musica mensurali	

INTRODUCTION

The first edition of *Tetrachordum Musices*, which is the basis of the present edition, was published at Nürnberg in 1511. As the title page indicates, it was written primarily for the school of St. Lorenz in Nürnberg, where Cochlaeus had become rector in 1510. The treatise quickly became popular, and between 1512 and 1526 six more editions were produced by printers of the town.

The musical contents of *Tetrachordum Musices* are derived, with certain important exceptions, from an earlier printed treatise entitled *Musica*, which exists in three editions. Each of these enlarges the contents of the preceding edition. In chronological order they are:

1. *Musica*, an anonymous treatise now at the Vienna Nationalbibliothek. A publisher, place of publication, and date are lacking.[1]

2. *Musica*, an anonymous treatise that has been the property of the University of Leipzig since 1507. It also lacks information on a publisher, place of publication, and date.[2]

3. *Musica* by J. Wendelstein, printed in 1507 at Cologne by Johannes Landen. On the title page a poem by the Florentine poet Remaclus includes the humanistic version of the author's name, Johannes Cocleus.

Mantuani[3] has proven conclusively that Cochlaeus is the author of the three prints, and that each edition of *Musica* is a development of the preceding one, beginning with 25 chapters in the Vienna *Musica*, then growing to 31 chapters in the Leipzig *Musica*, and finally reaching the Cologne *Musica* of 1507 with its 57 chapters. The Leipzig *Musica* must also have been printed by Landen in Cologne, since both the font of the print and the wood blocks of musical examples are the same as the Cologne imprint of 1507. Cochleus owned the wood blocks and gave them in turn to various printers of later editions. In this way many musical examples of these two editions appear also in *Tetrachordum Musices* of 1511, as well as in its subsequent editions.

[1] See J. Mantuani, "Ein unbekanntes Druckwerk," in *Mitteilungen des österreichischen Verein für Bibliothekswesen*, VI, 1902, p. 7.

[2] It is the *Anonymi Introductorium Musicae*, ed. by H. Riemann, in *MfM* XXIX (1897), p. 147ff., and XXX (1898), p. 1ff. [3] *Op. cit.*

Since neither the Vienna *Musica* nor the Leipzig *Musica* contains a date of publication, an exact date is a matter of conjecture. Mantuani suggested 1499-1504 as a possible time span for the publication of the Vienna *Musica*. Several modern writers have accepted as fact the idea that a treatise by Cochlaeus was published before 1501. As a result Cochlaeus has been given an undeserved position as a musical source for Wollick's *Opus Aureum*, and for this reason the origin of some of the contents of *Tetrachordum Musices* has been obscured.

H. Hüschen states that the Vienna *Musica* was printed between 1496 and 1504[4], and K. Niemöller[5] considers one of the anonymous *Musica* of Cochlaeus to be a source of *Opus Aureum* (*pars* I, II by N. Wollick and *pars* III, IV by M. Schanppecher), published at Cologne in 1501.[6] Since the relation of *Opus Aureum* to the three editions of *Musica* and to *Tetrachordum Musices* is very close, not only in regard to textual information but also to the numerous musical examples which appear in identical form in all these prints, it is essential to know whether the original material was the work of Cochlaeus or of Wollick and Schanppecher.

It is possible to eliminate the Leipzig *Musica* from consideration as the original source. As already mentioned, it was printed at Cologne by Johannes Landen. A clue to its date is given by an entry made on the final page: *Dono dedit quidam baccalaureus tunc temporis magistrandus MDVII.* Since Cochlaeus entered the University of Cologne in 1504 and was already a *baccalaureus* in 1505, the latter date could serve as the *terminus ad quem* of the anonymous *Musica*.[7]

Through a close examination of the Vienna *Musica*, its subsequent editions, and *Opus Aureum*, it can be shown conclusively which of these treatises is the original. On fols. B iv^{v}-C i^{r} of *Opus Aureum* (see Appendix III) Wollick prints seven exercises based on the seven hexachords of the complete gamut. The Vienna *Musica* (see p. 93) contains a handwritten version of these exercises that is identical except for several small but

[4] In the article "Cochlaeus", in *MGG* II, col. 1521. In 1496 Cochlaeus was 17 years old.

[5] "Die Musica figurativa des Melchior Schanppecher", in *Beiträge zur rheinischen Musikgeschichte* 50, p. II; "Wollick", in *MGG* XIV, col. 837. *Musica figurativa* is *pars* III, IV of *Opus Aureum*.

[6] For a modern edition of *pars* I, II, of *Opus Aureum*, see K. Niemöller, "Die Musica gregoriana des N. Wollick", in *Beiträge zur rheinischen Musikgeschichte*, 11 (1955).

[7] Both Mantuani, *op. cit.*, p. 19, and Hüschen, *op. cit.*, col. 1521, agree that the Leipzig *Musica* was printed between 1505 and 1506.

significant differences. One of these occurs in the exercise on the *C* hexachord, called *Primi Naturalis cantus Deductio* in *Opus Aureum*, and *Prime naturalis Tritura secunda* in *Musica*. In *Opus Aureum* the entire range of the hexachord or *deductio* is stated immediately in scale movements, and then the melody gradually descends in a logically sequential pattern. Near the beginning of this sequence the notes *A* to *F* are missing in the Vienna *Musica*. Again, at the end of the exercise, just preceding the final descending hexachord scale, three more notes are lacking in the Vienna *Musica* which are in *Opus Aureum* and which are necessary to conclude the rising sequence that had been established. Succeeding editions of *Musica* scrupulously follow these handwritten notes of the Vienna *Musica*, as does also *Tetrachordum Musices* (p. 41 of the present edition).

It is evident that Cochlaeus must have copied these exercises from *Opus Aureum*. His handwritten and printed versions are otherwise faithful to Wollick's treatise, and the omission of the notes mentioned above results in a much less logical melody. It is also worth noting that these exercises in his editions adhere very closely to the Gothic note formations and their placement in the *Opus Aureum* exercises.

Another much more subtle example of borrowing by Cochlaeus is found in the *differentiae* of tenors that are included in all his musical editions.[8] Without exception his *differentiae* are the same as those in *Opus Aureum*,[9] in which the *differentiae* are shown in a much more detailed manner. Wollick uses them as a part of a larger study in which each example begins with an *Euouae* and continues with antiphon incipits that are interspersed with various *differentiae*. His examples are lengthy and cover ten pages. Cochlaeus simply extracted the *differentiae* of each example,[10] collected them and then printed them as a unit on one page. It may be noticed that he has only one *differentia* for Tone 5, and for Tone 6, and none for Tone 2. This results from following exactly the procedure used in *Opus Aureum*.

Although many more examples, both textual and musical, could be

[8] On p. 52 of *Tetrachordum Musices*; f. D ii (*recte* B ii^r) of the Vienna *Musica* (handwritten); f. B ii^r of the Leipzig *Musica*; and f. B iv^r in *Musica* of 1507.

[9] Fols. E iii^v-F iv^r. See Appendix III, p. 94.

[10] In Tone 3 *Opus Aureum* has three *differentiae* and Cochlaeus has four. He accomplishes this by taking the opening *Euouae* of that mode in *Opus Aureum* and making it his final *differentia*. The handwritten *differentiae* in the Vienna *Musica* follow *Opus Aureum* exactly; the printed examples in later editions have two minor note changes.

adduced, it would seem sufficient if just two more were treated briefly. One concerns the formulas of the 8 Tones on p. 50 of this edition. These formulas, which also occur in the earlier Cochlaeus prints, are again based on musical examples in *Opus Aureum*.[11] Cochlaeus has taken the longer melodies of Wollick and formed his own by removing melodic segments from the original. Since the relation of these segments to specific places in the *Opus Aureum* melodies can be traced through each of the 8 Tones, the formation of Cochlaeus's melodies must have been made by a process of selection, somewhat like the manner in which he derived his *differentiae*. This is a significant point, since it indicates clearly that Cochlaeus, and not Wollick, did the borrowing. To consider that Wollick might have built his more extended and developed melodies around these particular *differentiae* and formulas of Cochlaeus is beyond plausibility.

A prominent case of a literal appropriation of music from *Opus Aureum*[12] occurs in the three-part compositions demonstrating *cantus durus*, *cantus mollis*, and *cantus fictus* (Exx. 1-3 in the present edition). Wollick printed these pieces in Gothic plainsong notation, which Cochlaeus adheres to in his editions. His Vienna *Musica* has notes only for Ex. 1, a handwritten tenor part which is incomplete, and a handwritten *discantus* which is complete and which follows Wollick's original faithfully. This *discantus* is the only completely accurate Cochlaeus version, for the later editions with printed notes in the *discantus* lack a repeated *a*, which is shown in Ex. 1 with a bracket.

From the preceding evidence it seems clear that *Opus Aureum* was an important source for all Cochlaeus editions of music. On this basis the possible time span for the printing of his Vienna *Musica* can be narrowed. Since Wollick's *Opus Aureum* did not appear until after May, 1501, when Wollick became a *magister* at the University of Cologne,[13] the Vienna *Musica* could hardly have been published before 1502. But Cochlaeus did not enter the University before April, 1504, which may have been the time of his first acquaintance with *Opus Aureum*. Yet it is possible that he had acquired a copy of it before this, for the treatise was designed as a university text book and enjoyed rather wide distribution. Before coming to Cologne

[11] The examples begin on f. E ii^{r}. See Appendix III, p. 95.
[12] Fol. C iv^{r}; also Niemöller, *op. cit.*, p. 39.
[13] Niemöller, *MGG* XIV, col. 836.

Cochlaeus studied at Nürnberg under Heinrich Grieninger, whose training must have been excellent, since Cochlaeus became a *baccalaureus* in 1505, a year after he entered the University. In any case, the Vienna *Musica* was probably printed between 1502-1504.

It is likely that Cochlaeus knew Wollick and Schanppecher, the co-authors of *Opus Aureum*, since they were at the University during part of Cochlaeus's period of study there.[14] Apparently all three studied music under Adam Folkmar von Boppard.[15] The fact that the Vienna and Leipzig editions of *Musica* were published anonymously by Cochlaeus might have been due to the presence of the authors of *Opus Aureum* and to the popularity of their treatise, since it already had several reprints during Cochlaeus's student days at the University. It was not until 1507, as a *magister*, that Cochlaeus identified himself as the author of *Musica*.

Although *Opus Aureum* is an important source of the *Musica* editions and *Tetrachordum Musices*, Cochlaeus by no means confined his borrowings to this treatise.[16] While he names the earlier writers of works he used, he did not acknowledge his indebtedness to later authors, particularly Adam von Fulda and Franchinus Gaffurius. The latter's *Practica Musicae*, printed at Milan in 1496, is an important source for Cochlaeus's sections on mensural music and counterpoint. For instance, his first rule of counterpoint in *Tetrachordum Musices* (p. 76), is an abbreviated quotation of Gaffurius's first contrapuntal rule, and his musical examples for the rule (Exx. 8a, b, c), are identical with those in *Practica Musicae*.[17] *Musica* of 1507 uses the Italian theorist's title and text in treating *De Consentanea suavitate quarta*, and borrows two musical examples from Gaffurius as illustrations.[18]

It is obvious that Cochlaeus demonstrated considerable ingenuity and a marked ability to assimilate material from various sources in creating his musical treatises. Not only do his musical works show a remarkable

[14] Schanppecher became a *baccalaureus* in 1497 and a *magister* in 1505; Wollick attained the *magister* grade in 1501, and did not leave the University before 1506. See Niemöller, *MGG* XI, col. 1597; also XIV, col. 836.

[15] Wollick ended *Opus Aureum* with a letter to Adam von Boppard, *sacre pagine licentiatus*, who directed the Cornelius bursa at the time.

[16] Appendix II outlines the probable sources of *Tetrachordum Musices*. While not attempting to be complete, it does point out verifiable sources.

[17] P. 124, Exx. 17a, b, c. Page and example numbers in Gaffurius's treatise refer to *Franchinus Gaffurius, Practica Musicae*, ed. by C. A. Miller (American Institute of Musicology, 1968).

[18] Fols. i^{v} and ii^{r} in *Musica* of 1507 contain the same examples as Exx. 23, 25 in *Practica Musicae*.

ability for synthesis, but they also develop continually in scope and content from the earliest, tentative treatise to his final musical effort, *Tetrachordum Musices*. One might relate the Vienna *Musica*, a kind of musical torso, to Cochlaeus the student; the Leipzig *Musica*, somewhat enlarged, to Cochlaeus the *baccalaureus*; the Cologne *Musica* of 1507, considerably developed, to Cochlaeus the *magister*; and *Tetrachordum Musices*, with its increased musical content that makes it the most valuable, to Cochlaeus the humanist.

Tetrachordum Musices is the second of a series of books written by Cochlaeus[19] in connection with his manifold duties at the school of St. Lorenz. The church's prior, Antonius Kress,[20] had embarked on a new curriculum for the school which would substitute a humanistically oriented education for the then current instruction based on medieval concepts. An influential adviser in this new plan of study was Willibald Pirckheimer, whom the town council had appointed to inspect the school. Pirckheimer had recommended Cochlaeus for the position of rector of the school of St. Lorenz, and Cochlaeus expresses his appreciation of the many kindnesses[21] of the famous humanist in the letter which prefaces book 4 of *Tetrachordum*. His comments on Pirckheimer's musical ability and the musical education of his children, as well as the latter's epigram to Cochlaeus on the title page of *Tetrachordum Musices*, point to a personal relationship which must have been influential on the development of Cochlaeus's humanistic tendencies.[22]

Tetrachordum Musices was written in dialog form for the school of St. Lorenz. In organizing his material Cochlaeus characteristically used his

[19] In 1511 he published *Quadrivium grammatices* and *Tetrachordum Musices*, in 1512 *Cosmographia Pomponii Mele*, *Meteorologia Aristotelis*, and *Brevis Germanie Descripio*. The latter book has been edited and translated by Karl Langosch (Darmstadt, 1960).

[20] A member of an old and distinguished Nürnberg family, he came to St. Lorenz from St. Clara's, a convent under Dominican rule, where he was prior. Two sisters of Willibald Pirckheimer, Charitas and Clara, and later his daughter Catherine, were abbesses of the convent. At St. Lorenz church Kress was not only prior but also a professional jurist. This was a requirement for priors of the two parish churches of St. Lorenz and St. Sebald, and points to the close relation of the clergy to the town council, which had patronage rights over the churches. See Gerald Strauss, *Nuremberg in the Sixteenth Century* (New York, 1966), p. 158f; also ADB XXVI, p. 817.

[21] Cochlaeus's indebtedness to the Pirckheimer family goes back to Johann Pirckheimer, the humanist's father, who helped educate the youthful Cochlaeus. The latter's zealousness in his duties at St. Lorenz also won the favor of Willibald Pirckheimer, whose nephews went to Italy in 1515 with Cochlaeus as their companion. See *MGG* II, col. 1520, and *ADB* IV, 381.

[22] In *Brevis Germanie Descriptio* Cochlaeus praises Pirckheimer's talents, saying his library was the best in Germany. See Langosch, *op. cit.*, p. 88.

latest *Musica*, the Cologne edition, as a basis, and changed its three sections[23] into four books or tracts. He accomplished this by expanding the first section of *Musica*, on plainsong, into the first three books of *Tetrachordum*, on musical elements, plainsong, and modes. The second and third parts of *Musica*, on mensural music and counterpoint, form the fourth book of *Tetrachordum*, entitled *Musice mensuralis principia*. It has been stated[24] that Cochlaeus intended his *Musica* of 1507 to be used as a university textbook and *Tetrachordum Musices* as an elementary book for the Latin school, because of the latter's expansion of material on plainsong and its exclusion of the study of counterpoint. This explanation, while pointing out the function of the books, tends to obscure a very significant relationship of the two treatises, which is that *Tetrachordum Musices* enlarges the musical scope of *Musica*, and that every important category discussed in *Musica* is also met with in the other work. For example, the study of counterpoint is found in *Tetrachordum Musices* on p. 76. It is not treated as elaborately as in *Musica*, but both the contrapuntal rules and muscial examples of *Musica* are included, as are also the three- and four-part cadence formulas.

Although Cochlaeus retains the essential elements of *Musica* in *Tetrachordum Musices*, the real value of the latter work lies in the material that it introduces for the first time. While his treatment of music in the various editions of *Musices* is strongly derivative, his treatise written at St. Lorenz contains his most significant personal contributions to music. They reflect a broadened musical interest and an understanding of current trends. Of particular note are the chapters on musical instruments, the four-part examples of psalmody, and the settings of hymns and classical poetry in four parts.

It is likely that Cochlaeus's interest in instruments results from personal ability as well as from his environment. Pirckheimer's epigram to him[25] indicates that Cochlaeus played the harp, while the latter praised his mentor's ability to play various musical instruments.[26] Nürnberg at this time enjoyed worldwide renown for the quality of its brass instruments,

[23] *Musica* does not have four parts, as Hüschen, *op. cit.*, maintains. The end of each section is clearly indicated, and the 1507 edition closes with: *Finis totius musice active, tris in partes divise.*

[24] Hüschen, *op. cit.*

[25] See title page.

[26] In the letter introducing Book IV.

due especially to the talents of the instrument maker, Johann Neuschel.[27] Cochlaeus relates[28] that he was personally acquainted with Neuschel, and praises him as a very skillful player and instrument maker. He further states that Neuschel frequently played the *tuba*[29] with his own choir at St. Lorenz church.

The two chapters on musical instruments that conclude Book I offer a survey both of historical instruments and of those in current use during Cochlaeus's lifetime. His sources of information, in addition to his own observations, are primarily Isadore, the pseudo-Jerome letter to Dardanus, and Jean Gerson. Of special value are his remarks on contemporary instruments, for many of which he gives both Latin and German names. His particular interest in the harp is shown in the title and treatment of chapter 10, and also the inclusion of Glarean's poem in praise of the harp, which concludes the chapter. To Cochlaeus the harp was the same instrument as the Greek cithara or lyre, and had great significance as a result. It was also the accepted instrument of many of the more enthusiastic humanists. Cochlaeus's predeliction for the instrument must have been strengthened during his stay in Cologne, where it was used by Hermann von dem Busche and Glarean, among others, in their humanistic poetry.

Of singular importance is Cochlaeus's comment about an English harp of his day with three rows of strings. This is probably an early reference to the Welsh triple harp, which has "three rows of gut strings, the outer rows being unisons in diatonic series, the inner the chromatic semitones."[30]

A significant contribution of *Tetrachordum Musices* is the four-part setting of psalm tones in plainsong notation. The practice of singing plainchant in a kind of chordal harmonization, but still retaining the original notation, was apparently well established, and is clearly shown in

[27] Among his patrons were Emperor Maximilian I and Pope Leo X. Burgkmair's woodcut of Neuschel playing the trombone with a group of fellow musicians may be seen in *The Triumph of Maximilian I*, ed. S. Appelbaum (New York, 1964), no. 20. While instrument making played a significant role in Nuremberg's fame at this time, it was only a part of the city's international reputation for all types of metal wares, whether utilitarian, scientific, or musical. See Strauss, *op. cit.*, p. 133ff.

[28] Langosch, *op. cit.*, p. 90.

[29] A trombone or trumpet, but most likely the former. See ftn. 14 in Book I.

[30] The article "Harp" in *Grove's Dictionary of Music and Musicians*, ed. E. Blom (London, 1954), IV, 91. A schematic representation of the three rows of strings may be seen in *MGG* V, col. 1550.

the three-part *Petre amas me* of *Opus Aureum*.[31] The same procedure was applied pedagogically to vocables in the hexachord system in the three-part examples of this treatise that Cochlaeus took over (Exx. 1-3). His four-part psalm-tone settings are a further development of that principle, and they must have been a highly important activity since, as he says, a choir sings nothing more frequently than psalms. In his five psalm-tone harmonizations (Ex. 9), one for each of the first five modes, he placed the plainsong melody in the tenor in each case except in Tone 4, where it is in the *discantus*. The melodies are essentially the same as the corresponding psalm-tone melodies applied to *Dixit dominus* in III, 6.[32]

As Cochlaeus's prefatory remarks to the four-part settings indicate, he intended the harmonizations to be formulas that could be sung to all lesser psalms. They could be performed either as plainsong or mensural compositions. Of particular interest is his suggestion for a ritard preceding the final harmony in psalm-tones using *tactus planus*.[33]

The reason that Cochlaeus made only five four-part settings and not one for each mode, is probably related to his activities as rector of the school. In numerous places in *Tetrachordum Musices* he speaks of the interference of other duties. Preceding his psalm-tone compositions, the four-part ode settings, and the poem to St. Catharine, he complains about the pressures of other activities and the necessity of doing creative work in a hasty manner.[34] Although his tenure at St. Lorenz was very productive, one can hardly escape the conclusion that Cochlaeus considered himself an overworked rector,[35] or at least as having so many obligations that he felt justified in constantly reminding the authorities of his manifold responsibilities.

One of the duties which apparently entailed much preparation was the

[31] F. C vi^{r}.

[32] P. 54.

[33] A procedure that Cochlaeus adopted from normal (monophonic) plainsong performance. A Psalter of 1537 contains the following rule: *Prima tamen penultima et ultima cantus notae, plus aliis protrahi possunt, ut cantores simul concorditer et incipere et finere valeant.* See K. Fellerer, "Regeln des Choralvortrags aus dem 16. Jahrundert," in *KJ* 34 (1950), p. 107.

[34] His remarks might also have been attempts to justify possible defects in his creative efforts. In Ex. 9, for instance, parallel fifths occur between *discantus* and *altus* in Tone 1 and Tone 4.

[35] Langosch, *op. cit.*, p. 162, contains particularly forthright comments by Cochlaeus on this point.

musical competition that took place on the feast day of St. Catherine.[36] Three Masses were celebrated on that day, at which the choirs of three schools and their respective rectors sang. Their performance was judged by a group of savants standing nearby. Cochlaeus asserted that no other German city surpassed Nürnberg in this kind of event, in which so many singers and such harmonious voices could be heard.

To conclude his treatise, Cochlaeus composed four-part musical settings of classical odes and religious hymns, in imitation of Tritonius's well known settings of Horatian odes, published at Augsburg in 1507. Cochlaeus must have been well acquainted with Tritonius's volume, and also with the humanistic ideas of the latter's teacher, Conrad Celtis, since Celtis frequently came to Nürnberg and was a friend of Pirckheimer.

Tetrachordum Musices shows the influence of Tritonius's publication in many ways. On its title page the opening text of thirteen lines is written in the form of an hourglass,[37] apparently an imitation of the earlier work, in which the title is set in the shape of a goblet.[38] Several poems follow, the first of which is an epigram of Pirckheimer to Cochlaeus. A similar pattern obtains in the other work, in which the first poem, *ad musophilos*, is by Celtis. The second poem in *Tetrachordum Musices* is of interest because it shows a personal connection with the work by Tritonius and with Celtis. The author of the poem is Benedictus Chelidonius of Nürnberg, who also wrote a Sapphic ode to Celtis that appeared in the 1507 publication of Tritonius. Chelidonius was a member of the Benedictine monastery of St. Aegidius,[39] Nürnberg's oldest monastic establishment, founded in 1140. He was a friend of Celtis and Cochlaeus, while his high regard of Pirckheimer was based primarily on the latter's fine reputation. A letter by Chelidonius in praise of Cochlaeus and Pirckheimer was printed by Cochlaeus at the end of his *Brevis Germaniae Descriptio* of 1512.[40] While Cheli-

[36] *Ibid.*, p. 92. Veneration of St. Catherine of Alexandria (feastday on Nov. 25), so popular in medieval times, continued in Cochlaeus's day. Every afternoon his choir sang the hymn that he wrote in her honor and published in the *Tetrachordum* (p. 86).

[37] See frontispiece.

[38] F. Waldner, "Petrus Tritonius und das älteste gedruckte katholische Gesangbuch," in *MfM* XXVII (1895), p. 14. Tritonius refers to his four-part settings as *harmoniae tetracenticae*; Cochlaeus calls them *tetraphoni*.

[39] He was also a poet, writer, theologian, and historian. His humanistic bent is shown in the appellation *Musophilus* which he adopted. See *NDB* III, p. 195.

[40] See Langosch, *op. cit.*, p. 166. Chelidonius's drama, *Voluptatis cum virtute disceptatio*, was performed at Vienna in 1515, with choral music provided by J. Diamond, continuing a practice begun by Celtis at the opening of the century. See *MGG* XIV, col. 607.

donius is a link between Tritonius's publication and Cochlaeus, it is undoubtedly Pirckheimer who was the greatest influence on Cochlaeus's musico-pedagogical endeavors. In these compositions his relation to Cochlaeus is similar to that of Celtis to Tritonius.

In the four-part settings of odes and hymns Cochlaeus follows the principles inaugurated by his predecessor. Each of the four examples in various poetic meters is in strict chordal style. The text is set with one syllable to each note,[41] and is printed for the superius only, in contradistinction to the odes in Tritonius, in which the complete text occurs in the tenor part. With regard to note values, rhythm, and mensuration, Cochlaeus differs somewhat from Tritonius. While the latter has breves and semibreves for long and short syllables,[42] Cochlaeus uses semibreves and minims. In addition, he frequently writes a dotted minim and fusa in place of two minims. Although he gives no mensuration signs in three of his four-part settings, they fit readily into *tempus imperfectum*. The other example, entitled Iambic Song, is in *tempus imperfectum cum prolatione perfecta*.

These homophonic pieces, functioning as a formulary method of learning poetic meters, are akin in principle to the preceding psalm tone settings. But in addition to their common pedagogical purpose, they bear witness to a new trend of the time, the developing consciousness of harmony, of a delight in the sheer sound of a series of full chordal structures. All four-part compositions (Exx. 9-13) in *Tetrachordum Musices* have that same harmonic characteristic in common. With the exception of the first and last chord of each piece, almost every other harmony is a complete chord, and the great majority are in root position. Just as the appeal of a continuous flow of solidly sonorous harmonies must have been considerable, so also the cultivation of such compositions undoubtedly had a significant influence in the trend toward a harmonic conception of music.

This edition of *Tetrachordum Musices* endeavors to present an accurate and smooth translation of Cochlaeus's text. His orthography in Latin

[41] Except in the elegiac couplets of Ex. 10, in which various adjustments are necessary. In the first line of the first couplet by Ovid, for example, *e* in *fragile* is elided because of the following *est*. In the second line, where *minor* falls on the second semibreve of the second phrase, the semibreve may be divided into two minims in all voice parts. In the same line a similar procedure may be applied to the first two syllables of *spacio*.

[42] In R. von Liliencron, "Die Horazischen Metren in deutschen Kompositionen des 16. Jahrhunderts", in *VfMw* III (1887), p. 49, the odes are transcribed without reduction.

humanistic poems, hymns, and classical poetry, has been retained. In certain terms, particularly of Latin and German instrumental names, both the original and modern equivalents are given. The Index and Chapter Headings are not in the original edition, which goes directly from the title page to the letter dedicated to Antonius Kress, and then to the text proper.

Diagrams, schemata, and monophonic musical examples are facsimile reproductions of the 1511 edition. Polyphonic music which is not in score in the original is transcribed into modern notation. If it is in score in the original it is reproduced in facsimile in this edition.

Exx. 1-3 and ex. 9 are transcriptions of three- and four-part pieces which were originally written in Gothic plainsong notation. In transcription blackened noteheads represent the Gothic neumes.

The poems by Pirckheimer, Chelidonius, and Glarean, as well as Cochlaeus's hexastich, which concludes this treatise, are facsimiles of the original. A nonmetrical translation is given in Appendix I.

Abbreviations:

ADB – *Allgemeine Deutsche Biographie*
AM – *Antiphonale monasticum pro diurnis horis*
H – *Hymnen* (I), in *Monumenta Monodica Medii Aevi*
KJ – *Kirchenmusikalisches Jahrbuch*
LU – *Liber Usualis*
MfM – *Monatshefte für Musikgeschichte*
MGG – *Die Musik in Geschichte und Gegenwart*
NBD – *Neue Deutsche Biographie*
PL – *Patrologia Latina*
VfMw – *Vierteljahrschrift für Musikwissenschaft*

CLEMENT A. MILLER

CHAPTER HEADINGS

TRACT I

Some General Elements of Music

TRACT II

Concerning Musica Plana

TRACT III

The Nature and Meaning of Tones

TRACT IV

Principles of Mensural Music

Chapter

Tetrachordum Musices by Johannes Cochlaeus,
Master of Arts from Bavaria and lately
active in Nürnberg, whose treatise,
now set in print in its first
edition and published
with divine aid,
is written
chiefly
for instruction
of the youth at the
church of St. Lorenz, but
also for the more profitable
and uncomplicated instruction of
others who are beginners in the art of music.

Epigram of Willibald Pirckheimer to Johannes Cochlaeus

Ingenium Cocles tribuit tibi docta Minerva
Deliciasque Venus, pulcher Apollo lyram
At numeros faciles varia et discrimina vocum
Mercurius pariter Thespiadumque chorus
Quid mirum superas si cunctos arte canendi
Cum faveant ceptis, numina tanta tuis.

* * *

Chelidonius Musophilus to the reader

Delius antistes Musarum carmen olympo
Concentu vario dulcisonoque canit
Quin pelago ludunt modulamina blanda canore
Sirenes, aer audit avesque suas
Necnon et letas numeris vocalibus odas
Orpheus Elisio personat, atque Linus
Cocles, Pieridum socius, iuvat arte Camenas
Pegaseumque melos percinit atque docet.

[Letter to Antonius Kress]

To the distinguished and pre-eminent Antonius Kress, renowned doctor of law, Prior at the church of St. Lorenz in Nürnberg, and most worthy in his own right, Johannes Cochlaeus extends heartiest greetings.

Most admirable Reverend Prior:

When in your beneficence I obtained a teaching position of authority, you charged me with the responsibility of three duties (may I never forget them). In the first (which you considered a principal and very salutary duty), the education of our youth in literature and morals should be holy and vigilant. In the second, ecclesiastical song should be studied diligently and completely. In the third, polyphonic music (which is very pleasing to our people) should not be neglected entirely.

With mindful disposition I accepted your precepts as if they had been brought forth from an ancient oracle of Hammon or Delos. I pondered each of them in my innermost thoughts, as I would strive with all my might to fulfill them. For this reason, since nothing is more pleasant, useful, and necessary than the common study of grammar and music, I then decided that I could laboriously write on both subjects. Indeed, the *Quadrivium Grammatices*, dedicated to you, has already been printed and is being taught to our youth, not without fruitful progress in the study of Latin (thanks be to God). The *Tetrachordum Musices*, a somewhat shorter but still compendious work that I have now written with hasty pen, in the midst of many other duties, is also dedicated to you, as was the *Quadrivium*. Each book tries to help young students with concise explanations rather than to display empty ostentation, so that in this way natural talent may be educated, the function of memory strengthened, and progress to more advanced studies may not be delayed.

Accordingly, this *Tetrachordum* is a compendium consisting of four short tracts, the first of which proceeds from the elements of music to the study of plainsong and vocal practice. The former, less productive than the latter, might accordingly be omitted from the primary education of young beginners. But the latter subjects contain absolutely nothing except the essentials; wherefore, they must be taught to students with greater zeal, so that they do not continue on to the priesthood without knowledge of music, always singing like laboring oxen, and, being ignorant of the rules of music, deriving no profit or enjoyment from such poor singing.

Therefore, most excellent Reverend Prior, I hope that you will also accept with benevolence this little book dedicated in such great measure to you, and that you may be persuaded that I and all my work are long since most devoted to you. Farewell, from our schools, June 24, in the year of salvation 1511.

FIRST TRACT OF COCHLAEUS'S *TETRACHORDUM*:

Some general elements of music

CHAPTER 1

Definition of Music

What is music? It is the science of modulating correctly, as Augustine states.[1] Or it is the ability to weigh differences of high and low sounds by sense and by reason, as Boethius says.[2] Or it is the knowledge of melodic species and those things that are related to melody, as Bacchius states.[3]

What is the source of the term music? According to some its source is: *Mois*,[4] which the Egyptians call water because it was found near water, and moisture is needed to produce a tone; or the nine Muses who preside over poetry and song, for ancient theologians on gods as Orpheus, and philosophers as Plato, wished the muses to be considered a concord of heavenly bodies; a muse (*musa*), a kind of high-pitched instrument, as a pipe (*tibia*), which is blown by human breath, or a cithara, which is played by hand, or an organ (*organum*), which is activated by bellows; or the Greek word *musa*, which means song (*cantus*). As Vergil writes, "Sylvestrem tenui musam meditaris avena"[5], and so Orpheus in *Hymns* believes that the muses are named by contraction from *Meluse*, for they seem to be nothing but *melos*, that is, harmonious song.

CHAPTER 2

Division of Music

How is music divided? Into three types. First, according to Richardus,[6] music is threefold, namely, mundane, human, and instrumental; each of these is divided into three parts.

[1] *De Musica*, in Migne, *Patrologia Latina*, XXXII, 1081.

[2] *De Musica*, V, 1.

[3] *Bachii Senioris, Introductorio Artis Musicae*, in Meibom, *Antiquae Musicae Autores Septem* (Amsterdam, 1652), I, 1.

[4] Concerning the etymology of *mois* and its relation to Moses, see Noel Swerdlow, "Musica Dicitur A Moys, Quod Est Aqua," *Journal of the American Musicological Society* XX (1967), p. 3.

[5] Ecologues I, 2.

[6] Richard of St. Victor (d. 1173), *Excerptionum Allegoricarum, lib.* I, *cap.* 10. Cochlaeus's entire first division of music follows Richard's text closely. It is in Migne, vol. 177, col. 198, but attributed to Hugo of St. Victor, although it is now considered to be by Richard. See J. Chatillon, "Le contenu... du 'Liber exceptionum'... de Richard de S. Victor", in *Revue du Moyen âge latin* IV, p. 23. Richard's chapter on music, nonetheless, comes from Hugo's *Eruditionis Didascalicae, lib.* II, cap. 13 (in Migne, vol. 176, col. 756).

Mundane music is threefold: one part consists of the elements of weights, numbers, and measurement, found both in their individual states and also mutually intermingled in composition and proportion; another part consists of planets as they are seen in varied aspects and influences in relation to their position, movement, and nature; and another consists of temporal values, as in years, months, and days, in the change and alternation of spring, summer, autumn, winter, of night and day, and of the waxing and waning of the moon.

Human music, which is also threefold, consists of the body, which has three parts: growth, temperaments, rational actions; the soul, with its faculties and virtues; and their union, in which a very natural alliance or harmony obtains, in that the soul is bound to the body, but is not in the bonds of the flesh.

Instrumental music, also threefold, is produced by striking, as drums and strings; by blowing, as trumpets and organs; and vocally, as in poems and songs.

The second division of music consists of two parts, natural and artificial. Natural music is twofold: mundane, which considers the harmony of the entire world and its parts, as well as the supercelestial and its elements; human, which considers the comparative relation of body and soul and of their interrelated parts.

Artificial music is threefold: rhythmic, which investigates word accents and whether a sound is placed well or poorly with words and syllables; metric, which investigates the measurement of metric genera in a precise and acceptable ratio; harmonic, which investigates the mutual difference and proportion of diverse sounds. St. Augustine has written judiciously on rhythm and meter in six books which he has entitled *De musica*. But here harmonic music will be treated according to an explanation of its scope.

The third division of music follows. Harmonic music is twofold: theoretical music considers the proportionate ratios of consonances, the unequal division of a whole tone, and the three genera of a tetrachord (*melos*). Boethius and Giorgio Valla[7] have described this music in five

[7] In "Musicae," from *De expetendis et fugiendis rebus opus* (Venice, 1501). For Glarean's opinion of Valla's work, see my edition of *Heinrich Glarean, Dodecachordon*, (American Institute of Musicology, 1965), I, 124, and *passim*.

books. Practical music relates to the practical application of sounds and consonances.

Practical music is also twofold: instrumental, in which diverse instruments are played; vocal, in which melody is produced by the human voice. Vocal music is twofold: ordinary (*usualis*), which lacks the principles by which it should be guided; regulated, which is supported by precepts. The latter is also twofold: *plana*, whose note values have equal measurement, and also move with the same intensity and speed; figural, whose note values are unequal, being subject to enlargement or decrease according to the indication of various signs.

The last division is appropriate to the present subject. The others, with their interrelated parts, are not treated here in general.

CHAPTER 3

The Subject of Music

What is the subject of music? A sonorous number. What is its proper medium? Consonance. What is a sonorous number? It is a number related to sound, or sound arranged in a numerical proportion.

Through related numbers music is investigated according to sound, just as numbers also refer to another subject. But arithmetic deals with numbers absolutely and individually. A musician considers *sesquialtera*, *sesquitertia*, *dupla*, etc., but an arithmetician considers two, three, four, and similar numbers.

Indeed, all four mathematical sciences are concerned with quantity, for arithmetic is concerned with absolute numerals, music with numerals related to each other, geometry with magnitudes individually and without motion, and astronomy with mobile magnitudes.

What are interrelated numerals? A numerical proportion which, when applied to sound, forms a consonance. For just as one number does not make a proportion, so one musical sound does not make a consonance. Thus two tones are required whose consonant size or interval is determined by an exact numerical proportion. For a fifth results from a *sesquialtera* proportion, an octave from *dupla*, and a fourth from *sesquitertia*.

CHAPTER 4

Consonance and Dissonance

What is consonance? It is a concord of mutually dissimilar tones brought together, or it is a numerical relationship of highness and lowness, for it arises from a proportional mixture of high and low sounds.

What is dissonance? It is the sharp and unpleasant clash of two tones which reach the ears as a mixture of incompatible sounds.

Consonances are either simple and primary, as a unison, third, fifth, sixth; repetitive and secondary, as an octave, tenth, twelfth, thirteenth; or triplicate and tertiary, as a fifteenth, seventeenth, nineteenth, and twentieth. Of these some are perfect, some are imperfect. Perfect consonances are the unison, fifth, and their octaves. Imperfect consonances are the third, sixth, and their octaves.

How do consonances differ? In two ways: first, a perfect consonance can stand alone, especially to begin and end a song, and an imperfect consonance cannot; second, several perfect consonances of the same species cannot ascend or descend in parallel motion without another consonance being placed in between. But many imperfect consonances of the same species can follow each other in ascending or descending. In order to clearly distinguish these intervals the following diagram is subjoined.

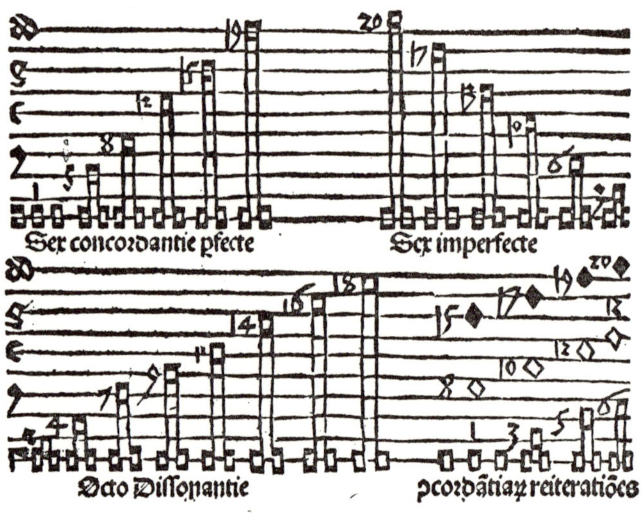

CHAPTER 5

Four Kinds of Musicians

What is a musician? It is someone who is skilled in those things that relate to melody. How many kinds of musicians are there? Four.

1. Those who are concerned with prose, and who express their thoughts in words rather than in melody. They are orators, lectors, and those who sing antiphons and psalms.
2. Those who not only express their thoughts, but who also declaim them in long and short syllables according to a metric plan, as in the case of poets.
3. Those devoted to the histrionic and mimic art, and who move with bodily gestures in imitation of musical sound.
4. Those who create sweet melody with mutually sonorous intervals. These are truly called musicians and singers.

But some wish to distinguish between a singer and a musician in the same way as between an orator and a rhetorician. For a singer brings to performance the musical concepts of a musician, just as an orator declaims in speech the rhetorical concepts of a rhetorician. Yet, just as one is not worthy to be called an orator unless he is also a rhetorician, so one should certainly not be considered a singer unless he is also a musician. Therefore, mimes and other performers of unskilful music are not really musicians.

CHAPTER 6

Sound and Vocal Tone

What is sound? It is anything that is specifically and solely perceptible by hearing. While sound is generally explained in this way, sound (*phthongus* in Greek) is the occurrence of a pleasing tone, that is, one which is melodically appropriate to a single pich,[8] or produced on one continuing pitch (*tenor*). *Tenor* signifies a tone that is held (*mora vocis*).

Both position and time occur in sound. Position is noted by the higher or lower pitches we produce. We call sounds on the same pitch

[8] From Boethius, *op. cit.*, I, 8.

homophonous or equisonant, and sounds on different pitches high and low. Modern musicians now generally call *phthongus* a note (*nota*) from the sign that is written, for a note is a tone intervallically suited to melody.

What is a vocal tone (*vox*)? It is a repercussion of air inhaled in the vocal artery and exhaled with resonance. This definition of a vocal tone is general and includes sounds made by animals.

According to Isadore,[9] an authentic tone in a melodic line should be high in order to reach the upper limits; strong, so that it does not waver and die away; pleasant, so that it does not offend the hearing; clear, in order to sooth and satisfy the ears; intense, in order to rise to the top which is called *alta* or acute; relaxed, in order to descend to the lower range, which is called *bassa* or grave.

The division of tone is twofold. The first division includes repetition of tones (*vocum repercussa*), in which a tone on the same letter name is repeated frequently; softening of tones (*vocum deficiens*), in which a tone is lightened in tension or relaxation; articulation of tones (*vocum articulata*), in which the thought is expressed distinctly; distortion of tones (*vocum confusa*), in which a tone cannot be comprehended in words or notes.

The second division[10] includes an indefinite tone (*vocum pedestris*), which we use in reading aloud and in making speeches; an inflected tone (*vocum equestris*), which we use to declaim poetry according to arsis and thesis; modulated tone (*vocum modulata*), in which we heed melodies rather than texts.

Equestris is clearly in the middle, for heroic poetry is not recited in a continuous manner, as prose, nor in the fluctuating and slower manner of a musical tone. Thus *pedestris* is continuous, but *modulata* is continuous with intervals. Therefore, the continuous movement of tone is called a discourse (*sermocinalis*),[11] but a melodic interval moves more slowly, so that its sound is heard more clearly, and it forms an interval not of silence, but of a fluctuating and rather slow melody.

[9] *Etymologiarum*, in Migne, *op. cit.*, vol. 82, 89A, 116A. In Cochlaeus's discussion of the division of tone, the meaning of *articulata* and *confusa* is clarified by reference to Isadore, who applied *articulata* to human sound, and *confusa* to sound produced by animals.

[10] This material is based on Gaffurius, *op. cit.*, p. 117.

[11] Cochlaeus probably had in mind the sermons or homilies found in the *Sermocinalis Liber*. See *Du Cange* VII, 438, col. 2.

CHAPTER 7

Intervals

What is an interval? It is the distance between a high and low sound. How many intervals are there? Fifteen, which should be learned in order from the subjoined examples and descriptions.

What is a unison? A repetition of one tone on the same pitch, as at (a). It is not a true interval in that there is no distance between a high and low sound. It is listed among the intervals because it initiates them, just as "one" is the beginning of numbers.

a

What is a whole tone? It is a complete step to the next note, as from *ut* to *re* and vice versa, from *re* to *mi* and vice versa, and likewise with the rest (except *mi fa*), as at (b). It is divided into these unequal parts: a larger semitone (called *apotome*), which is found between *fa* and *mi* on *b fa* ♮ *mi*, and which does not make a concordant movement; a smaller semitone (called *diesis*), which is found generally between *mi* and *fa*, as at (c).

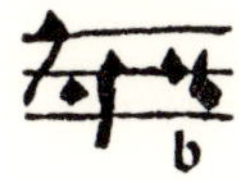
b

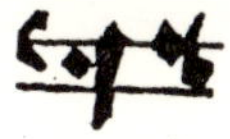
c

What is a *diesis*? It is the distance by which a *sesquitertia* proportion (a fourth) is larger than two whole tones, and is divided into two *diaschismata*. An *apotome* is divided into a *diesis* and a comma. A comma is the distance by which a *sesquioctava* proportion (a whole tone) is larger than two *dieses*. It is the smallest interval that can be comprehended by ear. As a result, a semitone is not called half of a whole tone, because a whole tone cannot be divided equally, but *semis* denotes imperfection here, as if a tone that is incomplete.

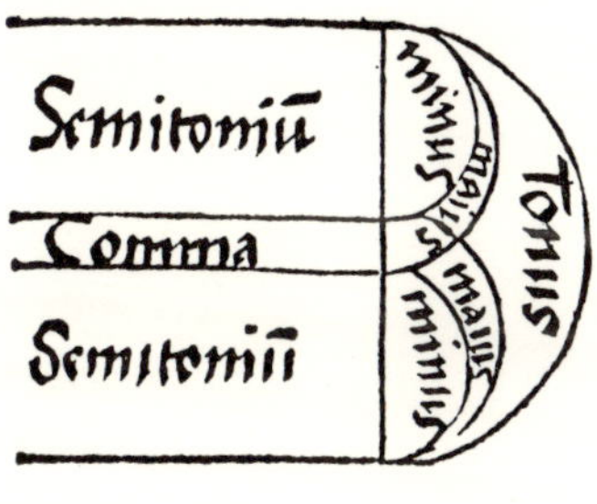

What is a major second (*ditonus*)? It is the distance of two whole tones. It is called a complete tone from *dia* (or two) and *tonus*, because it contains the distance of two tones, as between *ut* and *mi* and between *fa* and *la* in ascending or descending, as at (d).

d

What is a minor third (*semiditonus*)? It is the connection of a whole tone and a semitone, and is named from *semis*, as if an incomplete whole tone but not half of a whole tone, just as it occurs between *re* and *fa*, and also between *mi* and *sol*, as at (e).

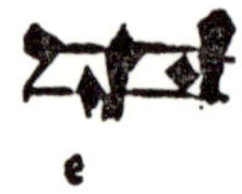

What is a perfect fourth (*diatessaron*)? An interval that is formed from two whole tones and a smaller semitone. It gets its name from *dia* (which is *de*), and *tessaron* or *quatuor*, as if consisting of four tones. It has three species, *re sol*, *mi la*, and *ut fa*, as at (f).

What is a tritone? An interval that contains three whole tones. The interval is not used on account of its sharpness, and it does not include a semitone. It occurs between *f fa ut* and hard *b fa* ♮ *mi*, also between soft *b fa* ♮ *mi* and *e la mi*, as at (g).

What is a perfect fifth (*diapente*)? An interval which contains three whole tones and one semitone. It receives it name from *dia* (that is, *de*), and *pente* (*quinque*), and extends from one tone to a tone a fifth away. It has four species: *re la*, *mi mi*, *fa fa*, *ut sol*, as at (h).

What is a diminished fifth (*semidiapente*)? An interval which contains two whole tones and two semitones. Its name is derived from *semi*, meaning diminished or imperfect, and occurs between ♮ *mi* and *f fa ut*. The interval is rare and unused, like the tritone and the diminished octave.

What is a major sixth (*tonus cum diapente*)? An interval which is formed from a whole tone and a perfect fifth, that is, from four whole tones and a smaller semitone. It is usually called a hard or major sixth, as at (k).

What is a minor sixth (*semitonium cum diapente*)? An interval which consists of three whole tones and two semitones. It occurs between *mi* and *fa* a minor sixth apart, as at (l).

What is a major seventh (*ditonus cum diapente*)? An interval which is formed from five whole tones and one semitone. It is commonly called a hard seventh, as at (m).

What is a minor seventh (*semiditonus cum diapente*)? An interval which is formed from four whole tones and two semitones. It is called a soft seventh, as at (n).

What is an octave (*diapason*)? An interval resulting from five whole tones and two semitones. It gets its name from *dia* (that is, *de*), and *pason* (*omne*). Since it includes all consonances and contains all pitches, of which there are seven, it forms the interval of an octave. Thus it is the most perfect of consonances, for it is formed in *proportio dupla* and arises from a fifth and a fourth. It has seven species, following the seven pitch names, as at (o).

What is a diminished octave (*semidiapason*)? An interval consisting of four whole tones and three semitones. Like an octave it occurs on the same letter name, but with *mi* placed against *fa*. Accordingly it is a dissonance, as at (p).

Other intervals which exceed an octave are equisonant to those within an octave, and are the same in nature, position, and difference.

CHAPTER 8

Three Genera of Modulating

What is a genus of modulating or melody? It is a certain division or disposition of a tetrachord or four tones. How many melodic genera are there? Three, the enharmonic, chromatic, and diatonic.

What is the enharmonic tetrachord? It is a progression of *diesis*, *diesis*, and a major third. A *diesis* is half of a smaller semitone. What is the chromatic tetrachord? It is a progression of semitone, semitone, and three semitones. The name comes from *chroma* or color. What is the diatonic tetrachord? It is a progression of whole tone, whole tone, and semitone, for it is named from two tones.

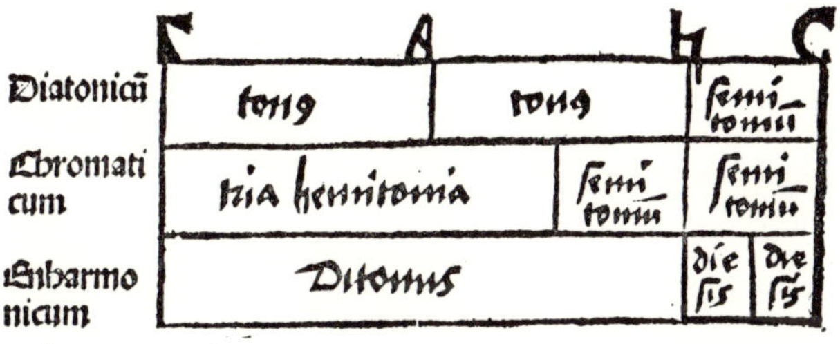

From these tetrachords we use only the diatonic, for it is more natural, since it is melodically suitable for all, even for the unskilled. The chromatic is more artistic and can only be formed melodically by erudite men. In former times the enharmonic was more significant; now only the most excellent musicians are able to teach and understand it, an ability that is denied to many. Its name is derived from *harmonia*, and formerly it was by far the foremost genus of modulating. But now it is greatly lacking in understanding and practice.

CHAPTER 9

Instrumental Music

What is instrumental music? Music that is played on various instruments. Its source is artificial music (*musica artificialis*), but mastery of it depends on manual dexterity, industriousness, and careful practice. Instruments are extremely varied in their shapes and manner of playing. Therefore, it seemed worthwhile now to speak about them and their characteristics. First we treat instruments which sound by blowing, striking, or activating bellows; then we treat instruments controlled by one's fingers.

Organ (*organum*) is a general term applied to all musical instruments.[12] But it is specifically applied to an instrument to which bellows are attached, by which air is blown into stannous pipes and sonorous tones are produced at a keyboard. In ancient times (as Jerome says), "a bag made of two elephant skins was attached, and a tremendous din was produced by fifteen pipes and twelve bellows, so that from Jerusalem to the Mount of Olives a sound like the clap of thunder was heard."[13]

If the organ pipes are made of wood the organ is usually called a positive. If the instrument is so small that one hand can play the keys and the other hand can manipulate the bellows, it is called a portative organ.

If there are no pipes or bellows, but if the keys are struck in connection with copper or iron strings, it is called a clavichord (*clavichordium*). If it has a softer resonance it is called a *symphonia*, but if it has greater sonority it is

[12] From Isadore, in Migne, *op. cit.*, vol. 82, 166B.

[13] In Migne, *op. cit.*, vol. 9, 219D. This (pseudo-Jerome) Epistle *ad Dardanum* differs from Cochlaeus's version somewhat, especially in the phrase (in Migne), "fifteen bellows and twelve copper pipes".

called a harpsichord (*clavicymbalum*). All these instruments are studied in the same way, and have the same tablature or representation of the music.

The most sonorous of instruments blown by human breath is the trumpet (*tuba*).[14] It is called *tuba* from *tubus*, which is a tube (*fistula*) or pipe (*canna*) through which water is drained from a tumor. But the trumpet has different shapes for differing usage. As Jerome says, "in one case it is used in connection with a gathering of people, in another a procession (*conductio*), or a victory",[15] or a solemn occasion. From the term trumpet (*tuba*) comes trumpet player (*tubicen*), one who plays a trumpet (in German *ein Trometer* or *Pusauner*). Formerly the trumpet was made either of animal horn or of wood, but now it is made of brass.

Types of trumpets are the *cornu*, *lituus*, *buccina*. The *cornu* is a curved trumpet (*tuba obtorta*), the *lituus* is a hooked trumpet (*tuba incurva*), and the *buccina* is a long straight trumpet (*tuba oblonga*). Those who play them are called respectively a *cornicen*, *liticen*, and *buccinator*. St. Jerome wished the *buccina* to be considered a derivative of *bucca* (the cheek).

The pipe (*tibia*) is also blown by human breath. It actually means the lower part of the leg, but it is used for *fistula* (pipe), because at first it was usually made from bones of deer or young mules. In German it is called a Schalmei (*ein schalmeyen*).

Calamus (a reed) and *avena* (a stem, stalk) are also synonyms for *fistula* or *cicuta* (hemlock stalk). From Vergil: *Tu calamos inflare leves*,[16] and *Sylvestrem tenui musam meditaris avena*.[17] *Arundo* (*harundo*, a reed) is also used to mean a simple *phystula*. A *monaulus* is a more sonorous *phystula*, a Zink (*ein zinck*) in German.

A bagpipe (*sambuca*) is now considered to be a pastoral and rustic instrument. It has many pipes of unequal length inserted in a windbag (as in bellows). The German name is Sackpfeife (*ein sackpfeuff*). In antiquity it was considered to be another instrument. In the current instrument dexterity is required to finger the holes of the pipes, although in trombones (*tubae*) greater skill is necessary in manipulating the in and out movement of the slide.

It only remains now to subjoin a few words on percussion instru-

[14] Cochlaeus uses *tuba* to indicate both trumpet and trombone.
[15] Migne, *op. cit.*, vol. 9, 220B.
[16] Ecologues V, 2.
[17] *Ibid.*, I, 2.

ments. A drum (*tympanum*) is an instrument whose one end is a hollow area covered smoothly with a skin that is struck with a small stick (*bacillum*). Gentiles were accustomed to use it in sacrifice to Cybele, mother of the gods. But now a skin that has been treated (*laborata*) is drawn smoothly over both ends, enclosing a circular space within the wooden sides. From *tympanum* comes the term *tympanista*, one who plays *tympana*. A *tympanistria* is a female player of *tympana*, and the verb *tympanizo* means to play *tympana*. A cymbal (*cymbalum acitabalum*)[18] was also used with a drum in sacrifices to the mother of the gods.

A sistrum is peculiar to Egypt, where it is used in the rites of Isis and sometimes also in war. It is played by women.[19]

A bell (*campana*) is an instrument suitable to be struck. Its clapper, which strikes the bell's side, is called a *baptillus*, or *ropalon* in Greek. Gerson has this distich about a bell: *Laudo Deum verum, plebem voco, congrego clerum/defunctos ploro, pestem fugo, festa decoro.*[20]

CHAPTER 10

The Harp and Other String Instruments

What is a harp (*cithara*)? An instrument in the shape of the letter delta. Is it different than a psaltery? Yes, a harp is played downwards, for it has the deeper strings at the lower end and all strings are fastened with small nails to the hollow side. But the psaltery is played from above, for it has the deeper strings above.[21] It has ten strings, all of which are stretched over the hollow soundbox which produces the sound.

The harp does not have a definite number of strings, but it generally has twenty-four (as Jerome says), and "is played by the fingers in diverse ways with varied tones and tinkling sounds."[22] Orpheus played a harp of only seven strings; on the other hand, the English at present are said to play a harp (*citharizare*) with three rows of strings.

[18] Probably from Isadore, *op. cit.*, 168 C, in his definition of cymbals: *Cymbala acitabula quaedam sunt, quae percussa invicem se tangunt, et sonum faciunt.*

[19] *Ibid.* A digest of Isadore's comments on the sistrum.

[20] I praise the true God, summon the people, assemble the clergy/toll for the dead, banish the plague, and ring out the holidays. From Gerson's *De canticorum originali ratione*, in *Libri et tractatus... Johannis Garson* (J. Koelhoeff, Cologne, 1483), vol. 3, f. 104r.

[21] From Gerson, *op. cit.*, f. 102v.

[22] Migne, *op. cit.*, 221 A. Cochlaeus omits *Pindar* in the phrase *per digitos Pindari.*

In addition, the psaltery has strings made of silver or an alloy of gold and silver (as Gerson says), which are plucked rather gently and which have a kind of tinkling sound.[23] But a harp gets its strings from a dead animal's intestines that have been dried, separated into strands (*subtiliati*), and twisted together.[24] The strings are also called *fides* and *fidicule*, although the word *fides*, *fidis* is often used for the harp itself. From *cithara* come *citharedus* and *citharista*; from *psalterium* comes *psaltes*, a male psalterist, and *psaltria*, a female psalterist.

The pick (*plectrum*) is the instrument used by a *citharedus* to strike or vibrate the strings. Martial: *Fervida ne trito tibi pollice pustula surgat: Exercent docilem garrula plectra lyram*. It is called a *pecten* by Vergil in *obloquitur numeris septem discrimina vocum, iamque eadem digitis, iam pectine pulsat eburno*.[25]

Some other instruments which resonate from the tension of strings are the lute (*testudo*), vielle (*viella*), *guiterna*, and hurdy-gurdy (*rota*). A *testudo*, commonly called a lute (*lutina*), has an oblong neck divided by frets (*certa interstitia*) and underneath a hollow, rounded, and very probuterant belly above which strings are attached. They extend beyond the neck to pegs (*clavuli*) affixed behind it.

The *guiterna* follows the lute's form although it does not have as large a belly.[26]

The vielle has a belly which is not as wide or protuberant, nor a neck as long, nor as many strings. It is also not plucked by the fingers of the right hand, as is the lute, but its strings are played upon by a bow, and thus produce a vibrant sound (*tinnitus*). But the strings are controlled by the touch of the fingers of the left hand, just as lute strings. In German the instrument is called a Geige (*ein geygen*).

The hurdy-gurdy (*rota*) is an instrument used by blind beggars. It has an enclosed small wheel smeared with rosin (*thure linita*) which a thick string touches and causes a sound. The string is controlled by some keys, like a clavichord.[27] It is usually, but incorrectly called a lyre (*lyra*), for

[23] *Op. cit.*, f. 102^{v}. The entire sentence comes from Gerson.

[24] *Ibid.*

[25] *Aeneid* VI, 646.

[26] Tinctoris calls the *ghiterra* or *ghiterna* a derivative of the lute and a Spanish instrument used by Catalan women. See K. Weinmann, *Johannes Tinctoris und sein unbekannter Traktat "De inventione et usu musicae"* (Tutzing, reprint 1961), pp. 42, 46.

[27] This description follows Gerson closely, but the latter calls the instrument a *symphonia*.

a Greek lyre is nothing but a cithara. It is undoubtedly from this that we speak of a lyric poem, for the latter is sung to a lyre, certainly not of beggars, but rather of citharists.

There is also an oblong instrument in the shape of a wooden beam, whose strings are played by a bow, like a vielle. In German the instrument is called a Trumscheit (*ein trumelscheit*), although some call it a *chorus*. But St. Jerome in a letter to Dardanus, has this to say about a *chorus*: "In ancient times the *chorus* was a simple skin with two copper pipes; through the first pipe the *chorus* received air and through the second it produced sound."[28] But now *chorus* means either the place singers occupy or a group of singers. And so these remarks on types of instruments are now completed.

Recently a friend from Cologne has dedicated a poem in praise of the harp to me. It is appropriate to add it at the end of this chapter,[29] since it is from a friend and is also a pleasing poem; moreover, it is most appropriate to our present subject.

[28] Migne, *op. cit.*, 221 D. Cf. Sachs, *op. cit.*, p. 281.

[29] Glarean, author of the poem, also uses it to conclude his own *Isagoge* of 1516 and his *Dodecachordon* of 1547.

In Dauidicũ Melos ac Cithare

laudẽ Carmẽ Panegyricũ: Henrici Glareani Helue-
tij: Agrippinensis philosophi: Ad Joannem
Codeũ Noricum

Gaudebam lepidas Cithara crepitante camenas
Tangere/et argute fila canora lyre
Cornibus argutũ tollit caput illa reduncis
Ceu cultos videas ludere sepe capros
Et querulũ collum clauo submugit eburno
Ventre latent blandi corpa mille soni
Admiror sonitus/equataq3 federa pacis
Cur medio summũ cõcinet atq3 graue
Murmurat ima graui/dum tangis/chorda susurro
Respondet gemitu pulsa suprema leui
Deniq3 que ex illis ficta est symphonia plectris
Mulceret fauces Cerbere seue tuas
Et num te reticem sacer et diuine poeta
O Dauid/querule sarcina sancta lyre
Munera dalmatico tua sunt maiora metallo
Et meliora tuis pigre Sabee focis
Orphea cõmemorãt Cithara traxisse leones
Et testudineo saxa fidisse sono
Te quoq3 cũ regno Pluto mulcebat opaco
Eurydicen cogit reddere sancta chelis
O quo te memorẽ versu dulcissime Arion
Ad cui⁹ pulsum monstra marina ruũt
Et Thamyras musis: contendit Marsia phoebo
Contendũt numeris ordine quiq3 soni
O quã dulce melos: Viuat iucũdus Joppas
Et cũ Terpandri Timotheea lyra
Stridula semifere Chironis Barbyta; nũquã
Dircei vatis carmina laude carent
Hoc sanctũ donũ/hoc nobis venerabile munus
A superis ceptũ/Tu quoq3 phoebe dabas
Et mihi persuasi/Citharam fore ab ethere lapsam
Quippe puto modulis pulchrius esse nihil.
Glareanus Cecini

SECOND TRACT OF COCHLAEUS'S *TETRACHORDUM*:

Concerning *Musica Plana*

CHAPTER 1

Musica Plana

What is *musica plana*? Music which keeps an equal measurement in its note values, without increase or decrease in their rate of speed. It is also called choral, since it is more truly familiar and frequent in choir and religious ceremonies. It is called Gregorian from its inventor, Pope Gregory. But St. Ambrose in large part has also developed this music, especially in the more pleasant modes. Thus religious song is aptly called Ambrosian by many.

This kind of music is especially concerned with musical elements, vocal practice, and the nature of the eight modes (*toni*). Its elements are threefold: the representation of song, as by notes; the recognition of song, as by clef signs; the expression of song, as by tones. It is fitting to consider these points first since they are fundamental, and the remaining later, but as no less important.

CHAPTER 2

Recognition of Notes

What is a note? A sign placed on a line or space by which the rise or fall of a melody is indicated. How many kinds of plainsong notes are there? Two, simple and composite. A simple note is one which is not connected to another; a composite note is one which is connected to another, as here:

Thus simple notes are more frequently applied to the text, since one syllable of text can be applied to every separate note. But in composite notes a text syllable can only be applied to the first note of a composite group. Therefore, the text should be written directly below the first note to which it applies, so that if many notes belong to one syllable, the first syllable should be placed under the first note and the succeeding notes should cohere as a unit. But if individual syllables are given to individual notes, the notes should be separated somewhat to give room for the text. In former times plainsong notes were written like mensural notes, with filled-in note shapes. Although they are still written as longs, breves, or semibreves, all of them receive an equal measurement of time, as one sees in this example:

A song can truly be notated with precision and clarity in these note shapes, and thus it becomes more nearly related to actual music than is the case with our note shapes. For this reason even now the same type of notation is observed in most countries, and in our country the monks preserve these note shapes.[1] But also in our notation the difference between oblong and quadrate notes should be observed, not because of temporal measurement (which is the same), but because of melodic rise and fall, and also of the application of a text. But this is learned more easily through practice and imitation than through precepts.

The distance between notes is indicated on lines and spaces. From a line to the next space is a second, to the next line a third, to the second space a fourth, to the third line a fifth, to the third space a sixth, to the fourth line a seventh, to the fourth space an octave (whose *termini* are always on a different line or space), to the fifth line a ninth, and so forth, as seen in this example:

[1] Cochlaeus's comments on Roman and Gothic notation are echoed by Glarean, *op. cit.*, I, 49.

Lines and spaces are numbered alternately. Just as line to line is a third, so also is space to space. The distance between notes is not affected by the width or narrowness of the space between two lines.

CHAPTER 3

Keys

What is a key (*clavis*)? It is the clue to a song. It is called a key either because it is placed (*clauditur*) on a line or space, or because a hidden and unseen key of a monochord shows us a pitch and tone.

How many keys are there? Twenty in the musical scale. This many surely suffice for the human voice, but many more can be added by frequent repetition of the same pitch names, as one can see in some organs.

The really essential keys are seven, following the seven letters, *A*, *B*, *C*, *D*, *E*, *F*, *G*. For when they are repeated they have the same nature and significance as the first letters, regardless of how many times they repeat the original letter. The poet Vergil has also written this in the lines from the sixth book of the Aeneid: *necnon Threiicius longa cum veste sacerdos*, *obloquitur numeris septem discrimina vocum*.

But keys having the same letter name, and an octave apart, are mutually different in three ways: first, by name, since some are low (*graves*) and some are high (*acutae*); second, by position, for some are on a line and some are on a space; third, by shape, since some are capital and others are small.

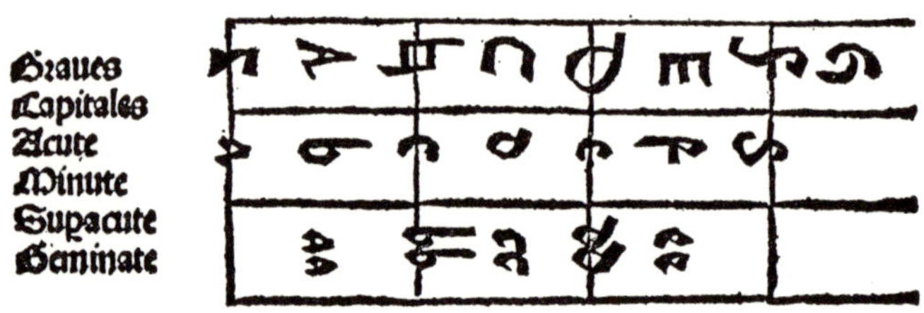

The above are the principal differences. Yet there are some other differences which we can call less basic: first, some keys are *finales*, some *confinales*, and some are neither *finales* nor *confinales*; second, some keys belong to one tone, some to two, and some to three; third, some keys are clef signs, others are not. Differences of this kind can be seen in the following diagram.

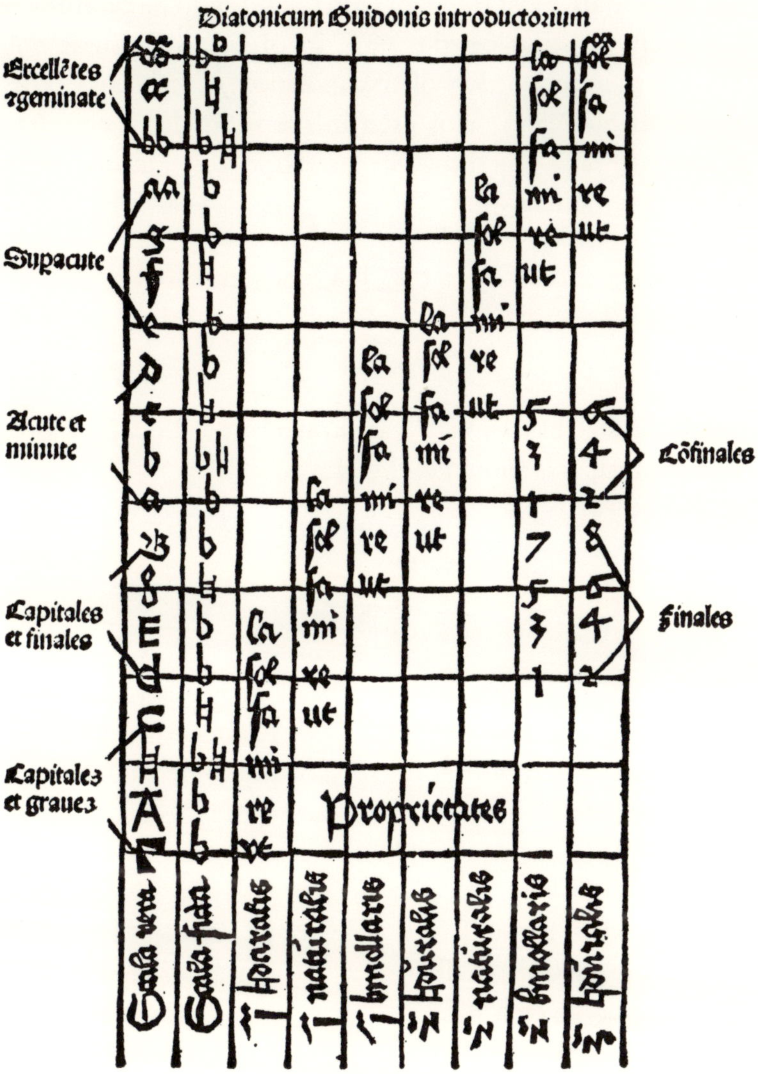

CHAPTER 4

Clef Signs

What is a clef sign (*clavis signata*)? It is a sign clearly placed at the beginning of a song. How many clef signs are there? Five. What are they? Γ *ut*, *F fa ut*, *c sol fa ut*, *g sol re ut*, and *dd la sol re*. The two extremes, Γ and *dd* are very rare, and *g* is also rarely used.

Thus *F* and *c* are most frequent, and they should be carefully observed, as well as their position on the staff, in order to facilitate solmization (*solfizatio*) and the recognition of transposition, if it occurs. They can be indicated in various ways, as is seen in the following examples. Among early musicians *F fa ut* was shown by a red line. In plainsong and mensural music it is shown in this way:

Among early musicians *c sol fa ut* was shown by a yellow line. In plainsong and mensural music it is shown in this way:

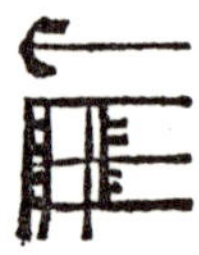

Early musicians indicated each *F* and each *c*, so that grave *F* was shown on a line and acute *f* on a space, but grave *C* on a space and acute *c* on a line. They indicated the twofold *b fa* by the color blue. Now, however, *b fa* ♮ *mi* is recognized by round *b* and square ♮, the former indicating *mi* and the latter *fa*. Yet *b fa* ♮ *mi* should not be counted among the clef signs, although it is written next to other clef signs. It was invented a long time after the other keys through the industry of Guido (as it is reported). All clef signs are placed on lines, and are mutually separated from each other by the interval of a fifth, except Γ to *F*, which is separated by a seventh.

CHAPTER 5

Transposition by Clef

What is transposition? It is the movement of a clef sign from line to line because of the rise and fall of a melody. Only clef signs are transposed because they alone are expressly indicated, although the other adjacent keys are also implicitly transposed, since the natural key series is unchangeable as it is found in the musical scale.

Thus transposition of clef signs has been invented so that an extended melodic rise and fall can be written on a few lines. When there are many staff lines, transposition is less frequent, so that it is rarely seen on a five-line staff, but it is more frequent on a four-line staff, since on a five-line staff the entire scale with three clef signs can be placed.

Just as mutation of tones should not occur unless necessary, neither should transposition of clef signs. For this reason it is more rarely found in mensural music, since five lines are always used and a sixth line is added to clarify the sequence of notes and their interval relationship.

For a correct and easy transposition these rules should be noted:

1. As much as a transposed clef ascends a subsequent note will descend, and as much as a clef descends a note will ascend, not according to position but according to its place in the melody in a given transposition.
2. If the transposed clef is the same clef sign as the prior clef, its higher or lower placement should be reckoned according to the position of the prior clef.
3. If the transposed clef is a different clef sign than the preceding clef, its higher or lower placement should not be considered in relation to the preceding clef, but in relation to the position of the transposed clef before its transposition.

But there is an easier method in which the singer observes the key on which the note preceding a transposition is placed, and then the key on which the note following a transposition is placed, and thus very easily recognizes (through knowledge of the musical scale) the interval between the notes, as these examples demonstrate.

CHAPTER 6

The Six Vocables

What is sound (*vox*)? It is air reverberated as exhaled breath.[2] What is a vocable (*vox musicalis*)? It is a syllable by which the pitch of a key is produced. How many vocables are there? Six, which are *ut*, *re*, *mi*, *fa*, *sol*, *la*, taken (as they say) from the hymn *Ut queant laxis* by using only the first syllable of a line. How do they differ? Two are soft, *ut* and *fa*; two are natural, *re* and *sol*; two are hard, *mi* and *la*. If this distinction is carefully observed it will make every song pleasant sounding.

There are three ways to sing: by solmization (*solfizando*), that is, singing syllables or note names; by singing the pitches of notes with their subjoined text; by producing sounds and tones alone, without text or *sol fa*.

The first way is suitable to musical tyros, for in this way they become accustomed to correct melody through the differentiation of tones. The second way applies to those accustomed to sing in a choir or elsewhere. The third way is appropriate for instruments.

CHAPTER 7

Properties of Tones

What is a property of tones? It is a diatonic and natural movement or progression of six syllables, either ascending or descending. How many properties of tones are there? In a genus there are three, and in a species there are seven, which is the same number of times that the six vocables are repeated in the scale. They can be repeated many times (as with organs) if more keys are added to the scale. They are usually called *cantus*, and they can be called hexachords, meaning six strings or tones.

What is *cantus*? It is hard ♮, which begins on G and which follows the hard scale with a whole tone between *re* and *mi*; soft *b*, which begins on F and which between *b fa* ♮ *mi* follows the soft scale, using a small semitone; natural, which begins on *C* and which does not ascend beyond *a la mi re* and does not reach the *b* key.

And so a *cantus* chooses hard ♮ from the *b* key if *mi* is used, and soft *b* if *fa* is used. The natural is neutral since it does not have *mi* and *fa* on the

[2] From Isadore, *op. cit.*, 165A.

same pitches. Thus there is a twofold key on letter *B*, ♮ *mi* and *b fa*. The first is called square ♮, the second round because of its shape. The first is also called hard, the second soft, according to their relation to *a la mi re*. Finally, the first is called ♮ *mi*, the second *b fa* from the tone that they represent.

The species of properties are seen very clearly in the scale. These lines are found concerning them: In *C* natural, *f* soft *b*, and *g* hard ♮, I will sing hard ♮ three times, and the other *cantus* twice each. The movement of individual species both by scale and by interval leap, is seen in the following examples.

CHAPTER 8

Mutation of Vocables

What is mutation? It is the change of one vocable (*vox*) into another on the same pitch. I call *vox* not a sound but a syllable, because the sound of each tone on the same key is the same, but the syllable and property are not the same. So one syllable changes into another and one property into another.

The two vocables *b fa* ♮ *mi* are not a unison, and a mutation cannot occur on them properly, for they are separated by an *apotome*, a larger semitone. This is evident, for *b fa* to *mi* on *a la mi re* forms a smaller semitone, while ♮ *mi* to *re* on *a la mi re* forms a whole tone. A whole tone is larger than a smaller semitone by an *apotome*. As a result, *b fa* ♮ *mi* is not one key, for all vocables on the same key are equal in quantity or size but different in quality or property, as Anselmus says in the third book of his *Musica*.[3]

A mutation is made for three reasons:

1. In order to make a more pleasant melodic transition, in which the quality of a tone is changed no less frequently than the size of the tone.
2. To permit tones to go above and below a hexachord.
3. To facilitate the exchange of a fourth and a fifth in a mixture of Tones, for each Tone normally comprises an octave.

How many rules of mutation are there? Three, based on three kinds of keys. The first kind of key has one vocable and no mutation; its four pitchers are *ee la*, ♮ *mi A re*, Γ *ut*. The second kind of key has two vocables and two mutations; its eight pitches are *C fa ut*, *D sol re*, *E la mi*, *F fa ut*, *e la mi*, *f fa ut*, *cc sol fa*, and *dd la sol*. The third kind of key has three vocables and six mutations;[4] its six pitches are *G sol re ut*, *a la mi re*, *c sol fa ut*, *d la sol re*, *g sol re ut*, and *aa la mi re*. But do not make a mutation unless it is necessary.

[3] It is highly doubtful that Cochlaeus had personal knowledge of Anselmi's *Musica*. His source is almost certainly Gaffurius. See my edition of the latter's *Practica Musicae*, p. 36.

[4] In his *Musica* of 1507 Cochlaeus lists the six mutations: in ascending, from first to second vocable, from first to third, from second to third; in descending, from third to second, from third to first, and from second to first.

CHAPTER 9

Mental Mutation of Vocables

What is a mental mutation? It means to sing one vocable and to keep the other in mind. This kind of mutation is more suitable than the prior kind, for singing both syllables means singing the same note twice, which is neither pleasing to the ears nor fitting in a song. Moreover, in mensural music it is completely intolerable, especially in smaller note values in which the speed of the notes does not allow a repetition of the same note. Thus explicit mutation is considered only as a beginning, but implicit mutation is its continuation and practical application.

To understand mutation four rules can be subjoined, one general rule and three specific rules:

1. When a mutation is imminent, it should begin on the third note before *fa* (if the third note is present), by ascending from *re*, or by descending from *la*. But if the third note is not present, the mutation can begin on the second or fourth note.
2. In ascending the hard *cantus*, *re* should be used on *d* and *a*, and in descending, *la* should be used on *a* and *e*, so that *mi* is always sung on *b fa* ♮ *mi*.
3. In ascending the soft *cantus*, *re* is used on *d* and *g*, and in descending, *la* is used on *d* and *a*, so that *fa* is placed on *b fa* ♮ *mi*.
4. In *cantus fictus*, *fa* should be used above all on *a* and *e*, and in this way a third is readily found on which *re* or *la* may be used.

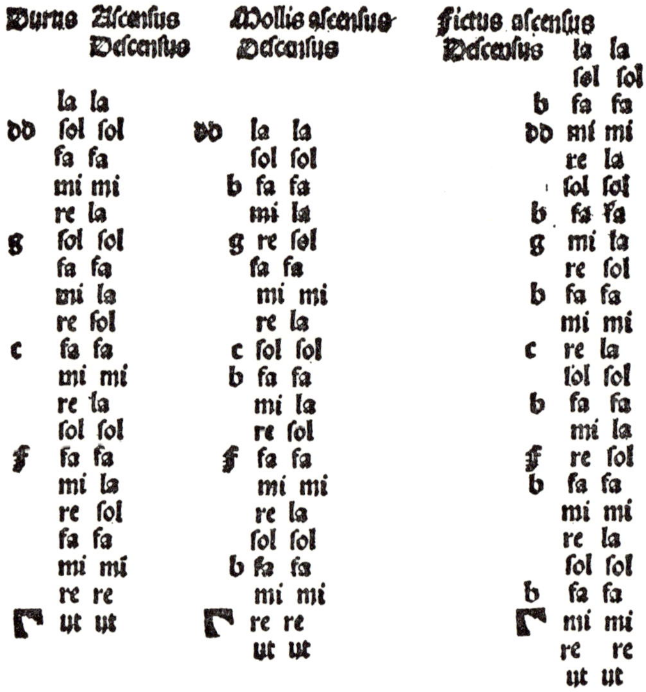

	Durus Ascensus Descensus		Mollis ascensus Descensus		Fictus ascensus Descensus
					la la
					sol sol
	la la			b	fa fa
dd	sol sol	dd	la la	dd	mi mi
	fa fa		sol sol		re la
	mi mi	b	fa fa		sol sol
	re la		mi la	b	fa fa
g	sol sol	g	re sol	g	mi la
	fa fa		fa fa		re sol
	mi la		mi mi	b	fa fa
	re sol		re la		mi mi
c	fa fa	c	sol sol	c	re la
	mi mi	b	fa fa		sol sol
	re la		mi la	b	fa fa
	sol sol		re sol		mi la
f	fa fa	f	fa fa	f	re sol
	mi la		mi mi	b	fa fa
	re sol		re la		mi mi
	fa fa		sol sol		re la
	mi mi	b	fa fa		sol sol
	re re		mi mi	b	fa fa
Γ	ut ut	Γ	re re	Γ	mi mi
			ut ut		re re
					ut ut

Ex. 1 Mutation of vocables in *cantus durus*

Ex. 2 Mutation of vocables in *cantus mollis*

Ex. 3 Mutation of vocables in *cantus fictus*

CHAPTER 10

Musica Ficta or False Tones

What is *musica ficta*? Music that is sung with false tones. Which tones are *fictae*? Those that are sung on some key to which they do not essentially belong, and also not to the octave key, as when *fa* is sung on *a la mi re* or *e la mi*.

But if a tone of this kind has a corresponding tone on the octave, it is a true tone, as when *la* is sung on *D sol re*, *sol* on *C fa ut*, and *fa* on ♮ *mi*, for these tones are expressly found on their octaves. Thus they are not *fictae*, since their octaves have the same nature, and are considered as the same.

Musica ficta is found most particularly between *mi* and *fa*, for if *mi* is sung in place of *fa* a whole tone is formed from a semitone, and if *fa* is sung in place of *mi*, a semitone is formed from a whole tone. This does not happen with other vocables, since they all form whole tones by moving in succession, and none form a semitone in the manner of *mi* to *fa*.

Therefore, wherever *musica ficta* is created, it is called a place of *coniuncta*, for a place of *coniuncta* occurs when we sing a whole tone in place of a semitone, and vice versa. Sometimes, because of the harshness of a song, we have recourse to soft *b*, without which there would certainly not be any pleasantness in music. But to avoid excessive softness in a song we turn to hard ♮.

If either *mi* or *fa* occurs on a key on which it does not naturally belong, or on its octave, it forms a *coniuncta*; but if it occurs on a key on which it belongs in the natural series, or at least on its octave, it does not form a *coniuncta*. Thus the same song transposed a fifth produces *musica ficta*, as here:

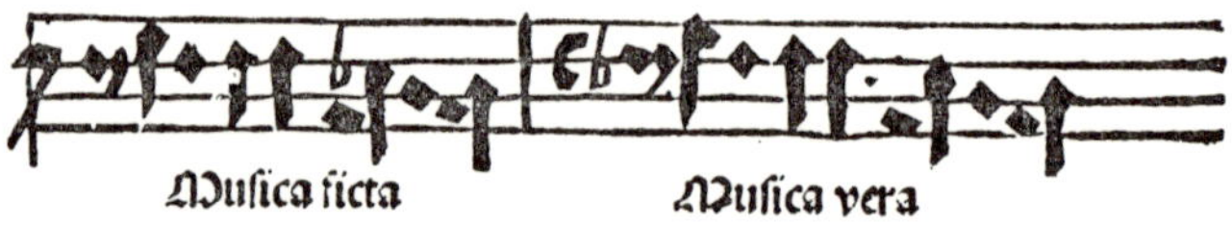

In order to avoid the unpleasant tritone, *musica ficta* often occurs on *e la mi*, for a tritone results if *fa* on *b* rises to an *e* on which *mi* is sung. But if *fa* is sung a natural fourth results. Moreover, a hidden *coniuncta* occurs in the *clausulae re*, *ut*, *re*, and *sol*, *fa*, *sol*, for a semitone is formed from a whole tone, as can be recognized clearly from the sound and from any instrument.

THIRD TRACT OF COCHLAEUS'S *TETRACHORDUM*:

The nature and meaning of Tones

CHAPTER 1

Definition and Division of Tones

What is a Tone (*Tonus*)? It is a rule determining the end of any song through the ambitus. It is called a mode, trope, constitution, and system. A system is the full range of a melody, as it were, consisting of the connection of consonances (a fourth and a fifth), for every Tone encompasses an octave.

How many Tones are there? Four among the Greeks: *protus*, *deuterus*, *tritus*, *tetrardus*, to which even now the four finals correspond. But Latins adopted eight, dividing each of the aforementioned into two Tones. They list them in a numerical order, while the Greeks named them according to the peoples who used them most. Their divisions are as follows: *Protus*, which contains Dorian, 1, moving in a serious, courtly manner, and Hypodorian, 2, moving with harsh severity; *Deuterus*, which contains Phrygian, 3, arising from the reviling of the impatient, and Hypophrygian, 4, moving with an air of flattery; *Tritus*, which contains Lydian, 5, moving with tempered liveliness, and Hypolydian, 6, moving with doleful moderation; *Tetrardus*, which contains Mixolydian, 7, moving with uncommon leaps, and Hypomixolydian, 8, following a modest and sedate course.

How is a Tone divided? Into authentic and plagal. What is an authentic Tone? One whose entire structure is placed above the final. What is a plagal Tone? One whose structure is placed partly above and partly below the final note, for it has a fifth above and a fourth below. Which Tones are called authentic? Those with uneven numbers, or 1, 3, 5, 7. Which are plagal? Those with even numbers, or 2, 4, 6, 8.

CHAPTER 2

Finals of Tones

How many final keys of Tones are there? Four, due to their combining in groups of twos. Thus an authentic and its plagal always end on the same key, following their original combination. Which keys are they? *D*. *E*, *F*, *G*, as can be seen earlier in the gamut.

Which keys are *confinales*? They are *a*, *b*, *c*. The seventh and eighth Tones sometimes have a *confinalis* on low *C*.

What is a final note or key? The lower note in the interval of a fifth. What is a *confinalis*? The upper note in the interval of a fifth, for a *confinalis* should be a fifth from its final. But when the seventh and eighth Tones end on *G*, they do not have a *confinalis* above because of the excessive highness of the keys. Sometimes, but rarely, they end on low *C*.

Yet in mensural music *confinales* are accepted at will as long as a song keeps the same consonance. In this way all Tones in figural song can avail themselves of a *confinalis* on the fourth above the final by singing *fa* on *b fa* ♮ *mi*. The systems of Tones can be understood from the subjoined notes.

You see, therefore, how an authentic Tone is divided on the *confinalis* and a plagal Tone is divided on the final. I call the median tone the one which divides a fifth and a fourth, and which is common to both. In authentic Tones, therefore, the final note is always the lowest, while in plagal Tones a fourth lies below it. So a song in an authentic Tone should not begin as high as its plagal begins.

CHAPTER 3

Range and Ambitus of Tones

What is the ambitus of a Tone? It is the distance that the rule of very Tone allows it to move, that is, how far each should ascend or descend from its final.

From this two rules result. First, every authentic Tone regularly ascends to the octave above the final, or more freely to the ninth or tenth above, and descends to a second below the final. Second, every plagal Tone regularly ascends to the fifth above the final note, or more freely to the sixth above, and regularly descends to the fourth below the final, or more freely to the fifth below. But the ambitus of each Tone regularly fills out an octave.

The ambitus of each authentic Tone is: Tone 1, from *D sol re* to *d la sol re*; Tone 3, from *E la mi* to *e la mi*; Tone 5, from *F fa ut* to *f fa ut*; Tone 7, from *G sol re ut* to *g sol re ut*.

The ambitus of each plagal Tone is: Tone 2, from *A re* to *a la mi re*; Tone 4, from ♮ *mi* to *b fa* ♮ *mi*; Tone 6, fom *C fa ut* to *c sol fa ut*; Tone 8, from *D sol re* to *d la sol re*.

An authentic Tone does not always reach its octave, or a plagal Tone its fifth, but it should be understood that they have the ability to do so. Sometimes a song uses the entire ambitus, sometimes it uses less, sometimes it exceeds the ambitus, and sometimes it uses the ambitus of an authentic and a plagal Tone. Thus the same Tone may accidentally have many names, as mixed, imperfect, pluperfect, and irregular.

What is a mixed Tone? One which contains the tetrachords of an authentic and plagal Tone, for an authentic and plagal Tone have a common fifth, but fourths which are separated and which are both included in a mixed Tone.

What is an imperfect Tone? One which does not fill out an entire octave, but is deficient in the fifth, or in the fourth, or in both.

What is a pluperfect Tone? One which ascends one or two notes beyond the octave if it is authentic, or descends one or two notes beyond the octave if it is plagal.

What is an irregular Tone? One which ends on its *confinalis*; for example, the first Tone regularly ends on *d sol re*, and irregularly on *a la mi re*.

An authentic Tone is also called commixed when it contains melodic types other than those of its plagal, and a plagal Tone is called commixed when it contains forms other than those of its principal.

CHAPTER 4

The Melodia of Tones

What is the *melodia* of a Tone? It is a normal progression of notes using a certain interval which is more common to one Tone than to another.[1] From an understanding of *melodia* four notes result, which follow the four finals of Tones.

1. A song beginning on *d sol re* which frequently moves from *re* to high *la* and also rises to *fa* above *la*, belongs to the first Tone. But if it is centered about *re* and frequently comes to *fa*, the third above, it belongs to the second Tone.

2. If a song originating on *e la mi* often reaches *la* a sixth above, it belongs to the third Tone. But if it moves more frequently from *mi* to *la* a fourth above, it belongs to the fourth Tone.

3. If a song beginning on *F fa ut* often moves from *ut* up to *sol*, back to *mi*, and again returns to *sol*, it belongs to the fifth Tone. But if it moves more frequently between *fa* and *la* a third above, it belongs to the sixth Tone.

4. A song beginning on *G sol re ut* which often rises from *ut* to *sol* and reaches *la* above, belongs to the seventh Tone. But if *ut* rises to *fa* more often, and *fa* is reached by descending a fifth, the song belongs to the eighth Tone.

A verse: first, *re la*; second, *re fa*; third, *mi fa*; fourth, *mi la*; fifth, *fa sol*; sixth, *fa la*; seventh, *ut sol*; eighth, *ut fa*. Examples follow.

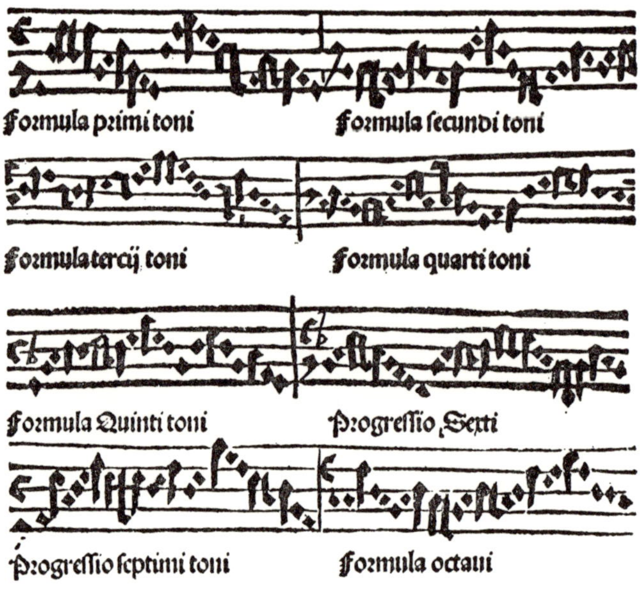

[1] *Melodia* in Cochlaeus is equivalent to Glarean's *phrasis*. See Miller, *op. cit.*, I, 195, and *passim*.

If the preceding discussion has been considered carefully, one can easily recognize the Tone to which a song belongs through hearing alone, even if the notes have not been examined. For this reason every one should observe the *melodia* with the greatest care, since an authentic Tone does not differ from its plagal in its final, or in the quality of a song, but in the *melodia* and ascent and descent.

But Tones are also different in the quality or property of a song, for in the fifth and sixth Tones *fa* is always sung on the *b* key, while all the other Tones require *mi* on that key. Moreover, in the first and second Tones *fa* is sung on *b* when the melody rises a single note above *a la mi re*, but when it rises more notes above *a la mi re*, *mi* is sung.

Similarly, when the fifth and sixth Tones begin on *F fa ut*, *fa* is sung on the *b* key. If by transposition they end on *c sol fa ut*, *mi* is sung on *b fa ♮ mi*, just as previously *mi* was sung on *e la mi*.

CHAPTER 5

The Tenor and Differentiae of Tones

What is a tenor? In religious songs it is a rather short melody at the end of which the letters *Euouae* are subjoined. *Euouae* indicate *seculorum Amen* by omitting the consonants. The words *saeculorum Amen* occur at the end of the *Gloria patri*, which Pope Damascus I, following the counsel of St. Jerome, ordained to be sung at the end of Psalms. The word tenor comes from *tenendus*, because it keeps a song from wandering from its own Tone to another.

How many tenors are there? Two, a tenor of antiphons and a tenor of introits. What is a tenor of antiphons? A melody according to which the endings of psalms are completed. What is a tenor of introits? A melody according to which the endings of verses are completed. There are as many tenors of antiphons and introits as there are Tones.

Some tenors are changed by certain variations in the *differentiae* of Tones, in order to make the beginning of a song easier, for the pitch which begins a song is not always the same pitch as at the end. Therefore the principal tenor note is chosen according to the end, and *differentiae* are chosen according to the beginning.

Differentiae do not exist because of necessity, for any song can be sung according to the principal tenor note, but in order to prepare a smoother and easier transition to the beginning of a song. Since the endings of a song are made according to the pleasure of a singer rather than according to a rule, they are selected in different ways by different singers.

It is not necessary to spend a great deal of time on them, since they are certainly not the same among all singers, and since they are always indicated at the ends of the antiphons. In liturgical books they are shown in an abbreviated way by two or three notes, the number of the Tone is added, and thus the tenor is easily discovered.

It seems unnecessary to indicate the initial keys of any Tone, since they are not definite and limited, and since a particular *differentia* of a tenor does not correspond to any particular Tone. So it is enough to carefully observe the principal tenors, although it is also appropriate to touch upon some forms of *differentiae*. Tenors of antiphons and their *differentiae* follow.

CHAPTER 6

Psalmody of Tones

What is psalmody? It is singing of psalms according to the tenors of Tones. How many kinds are there? Two, major and minor.

What is major psalmody? Psalmody which varies the intonation and mediation with a more ornate melody, and which ends on the tenor of a Tone. Which are the major psalms? The Magnificat and the Benedictus, the canticles (I say) of Mary and Zachary.

What is minor psalmody? Psalmody which has a more simple intonation, a varied mediation, and a termination on the tenor of a Tone. Which are minor psalms? All psalms except the Magnificat and the Benedictus. Although *In exitu Israel de Egypto*, the canticle of Moses, and the *Te Deum laudamus*, the song of Ambrose and Augustine, seem to be far from minor psalms and to approach major psalms more closely, the same psalm melodies cannot be used for them. Therefore, the following rules of psalmody must be observed.

1. No psalmody should begin on a note higher than the corresponding note at the beginning of the *Euouae*. So the tenor of an authentic Tone always begins more than a fourth above the final, on the fifth or sixth, and the tenor of a plagal Tone always begins less than a fifth above the final, on the third or fourth, as will be seen in the subjoined examples.
2. In psalms a mediation ends with two kinds of pauses, unchanged (*integra*) and altered (*corrupta*). A pause is unchanged when it keeps the formula of a Tone, and altered when, contrary to the formula of a Tone, it rises at the close of the mediation. Which pauses are called altered? They are: all Hebraic words, such as *Syon*, *Hierusalem*, *Cedar*; monosyllabic words, as *me*, *te*, *fac*; indeclinable words, as *Israhel*.
3. Some Tones share the same mediation, but never the same final. For example, in minor psalms the first and sixth Tones favor the same mediation. In major psalms the first and sixth Tones have the same intonation, and also the second and eighth Tones. Examples of psalmody follow.

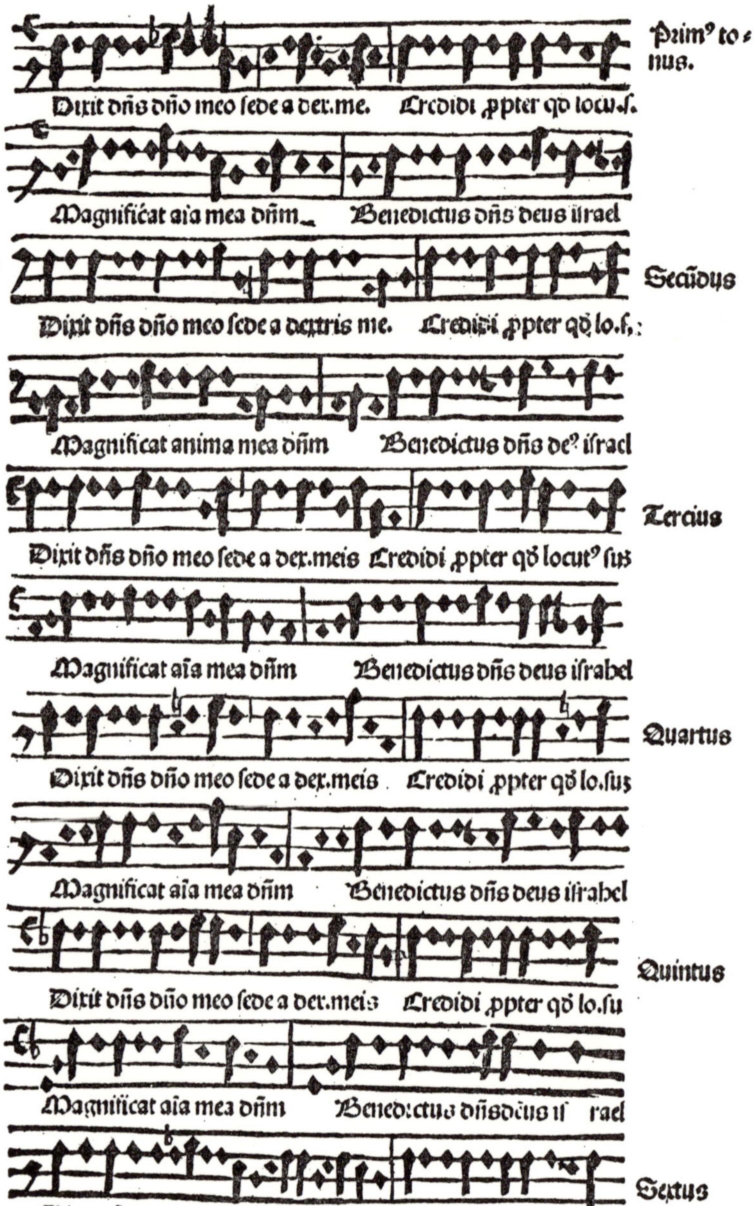
Prim⁹ tonus.
Dixit dñs dño meo sede a dex.me. Credidi ꝓpter qd locu.s.
Magnificat aïa mea dñm. Benedictus dñs deus israel
Secũdus
Dixit dñs dño meo sede a dextris me. Credidi ꝓpter qd lo.s.
Magnificat anima mea dñm Benedictus dñs de⁹ israel
Tercius
Dixit dñs dño meo sede a dex.meis Credidi ꝓpter qd locut⁹ sũ
Magnificat aïa mea dñm Benedictus dñs deus israhel
Quartus
Dixit dñs dño meo sede a dex.meis Credidi ꝓpter qd lo.sũ
Magnificat aïa mea dñm Benedictus dñs deus israhel
Quintus
Dixit dñs dño meo sede a dex.meis Credidi ꝓpter qd lo.sũ
Magnificat aïa mea dñm Benedictus dñs deus is rael
Sextus
Dixit dñs dño meo sede a dex.meis Credidi ꝓpter qd lo.sũ

CHAPTER 7

Tenors of Introits

What is an introit? [A Mass part] accompanying the entrance of the priest to the Sacrifice at the altar. For use at the introit of the Mass, Pope Celestine assigned the one hundred fifty psalms of David to be chanted antiphonally. All regular introits, graduals, offertories, and post communions are taken from them (as it is written in *Rationale divinorum* IV, 5).[2] But Gregory arranged the introit of the Mass with song and retained one verse from the psalm which previously was sung in full.

What are tenors of introits? Those which are sung up to the end of verses which are subscribed with *Euouae*. They are always indicated in full, never in abbreviated form (as in some places in psalm tenors). But they admit some variation in *differentiae* to facilitate a smoother and easier repetition of the introit.

[2] Cochlaeus has IV, 51. *Rationale Divinorum Officiorum*, an authoritative and comprehensive medieval treatise on liturgical rites, vestments, etc., and their symbolism, was written in 1286 by Gulielmus Durandus (Duranti, Durantis), bishop of Mende. The treatise was first printed at Mainz in 1459, and reprinted many times thereafter.

The Tone of an introit is not found from the final of the verse, but from the true final which occurs before the verse. Thus a verse follows the Tone of its introit, and not the opposite. In this way the Tone of introits is recognized properly and in particular from its final. But it is also understood by inference, so to speak, from the *melodiae* of verses. Verse formulas in eight Tones follow.

CHAPTER 8

Verse Responsories in Eight Tones

What is a responsory? A chant formed from a beginning part, a repeated part, and a verse. It is a response to the capitulum in Vespers or the lection in Matins. A responsory has a varied melodic movement up to the verse, which maintains a melodic formula in some Tone.

The repeated part should be arranged so that the verse may begin smoothly after it, and so that it may then follow the verse with suitable regard for melodic smoothness and textual meaning. Verse formulas can be studied in eight melodies based on the eight Tones. Although the *Gloria patri* formulas do not change, verse formulas vary because their texts differ in length.

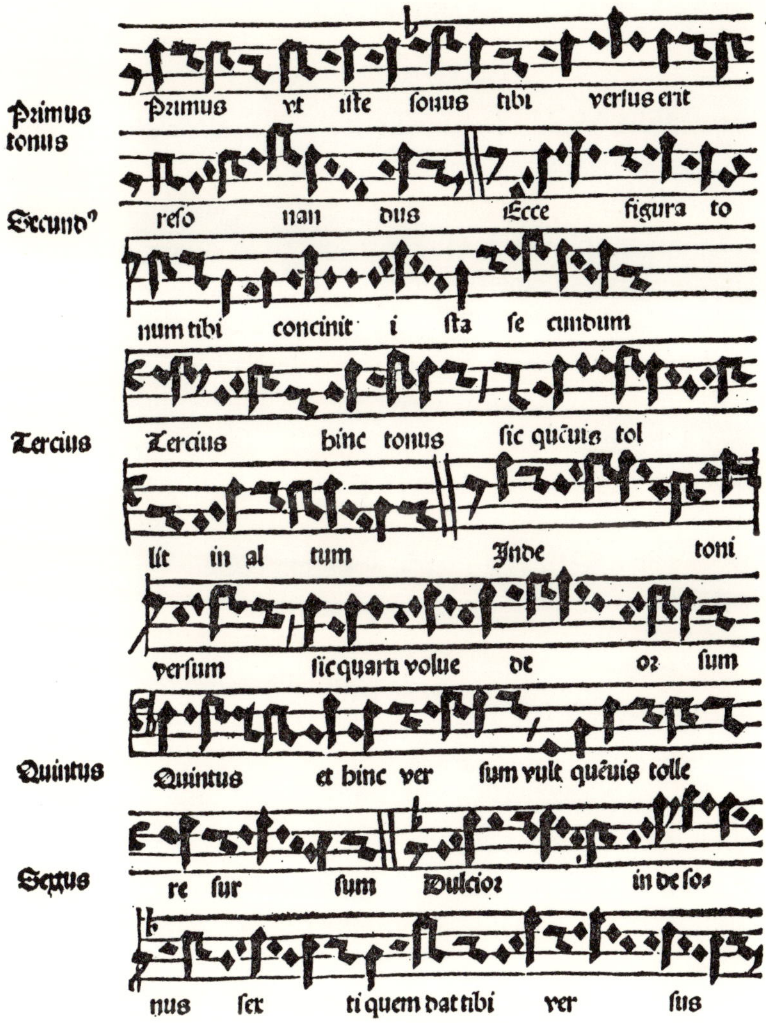

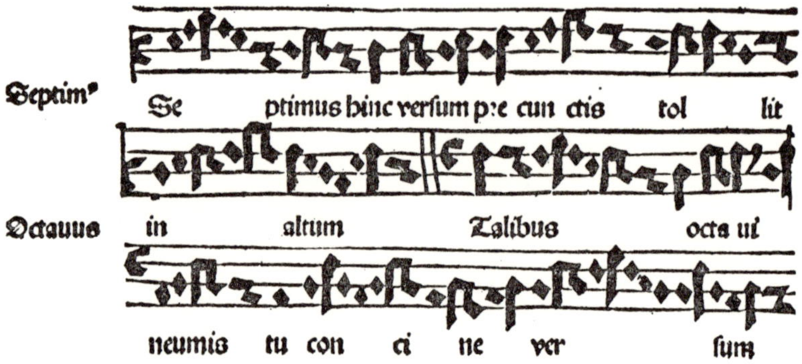

CHAPTER 9

Remaining Kinds of Chant

What are the kinds of chant in ecclesiastical or choral music? Antiphons, responsories, hymns, introits, graduals, alleluias, sequences, and also some other chants, as offertory, *Kyrie eleison*, and so forth.

What is an antiphon? A song introduced in divine praises to refresh one. Its meaning is explained variously as sounding *ante psalmum*, because the psalm's melody is formed in accordance with its tone; from *anti*, or before, and *phonos* or sound, because a psalm is intoned according to its melody; according to Isadore, antiphon is a Greek word meaning alternating sound, because two choirs alternate in singing the psalm (*cantus*) of the melodies. A responsory relates to the verse (*historia*) as an antiphon to psalms, as previously mentioned.

What is a hymn? It is a metric song expressing praise of God. Distinguished authors of hymns were Orpheus among the pagans and Hilary, Bishop of Poitiers and Ambrose, Bishop of Milan, among the Christians. Various poetic genera are allowed, especially sapphic, iambic, and choriambic, as in *vita sanctorum*, *veni creator spiritus*, and *festum nunc celebre*. Introits have been discussed earlier.

What is a gradual? It is a chant which is called the responsory of the epistle, since it has a verse but is not repeated after the verse. It should not begin on a high pitch because its verse ascends still higher. A gradual is named from *gradus* because it was formerly sung from the steps of the altar.

What is an alleluia? It is a song of jubilation raising the mind to contemplation of God. The word is Hebraic and is equivalent to the Latin *laudate dominum*, or let all praise the Lord. For Jerome says that *allelu* is a verb in the imperative mood, and that *yia* means universal.

What is a sequence? It is a chant with a laudatory text and pleasant melody. It is also called *prosa* because of its prose style (*soluta oratio*), and sequence because it follows the neume of the *jubilus* or alleluia. Its inventor is Notherus, abbot of St. Gall, and it was allowed to be sung at Mass by Pope Nicholas. There are also kinds of melody whose neumes should be carefully distinguished.

What is a neume? It is a series of tones or notes which are suitable to be sung in one breath. As Guido says, a neume should begin and end where most frequently and easily the tone on which it occurs can be chosen to begin again. This is shown by a line drawn through all staff lines in the manner of a rest, as here:

CHAPTER 10

Recitation Tones

How many kinds of recitation tones are there? Three, in Epistles, Prophecies, and Collects respectively. What is a collect? A prayer said before the collected people. Its recitation is even and always on the same note.

What is an Epistle? A letter sent by the Apostles to absent brethren who were sent out to preach the gospel, that is, the good news. The recitation tones of Epistles and Gospels are the same, although in different localities they vary in their pitch. Everywhere, however, an interrogation raises the last note a step, just as it is also raised at the end. For in the New Testament the celestial and not the earthly is promised to us.

What is a Prophecy? A prayer taken from the Old Testament. What is its recitation tone? It usually has two kinds, for in some prayers the final note is raised at the *virgula*, and in others the pitch of the preceding notes is kept. But at a *comma* there is always a descent of a third, unless the word is monosyllabic, Hebraic, or indeclinable. The latter kind of word tends to be raised, just as it is raised in psalmody, contrary to the nature of the Tone. An interrogation is always raised, and a *colon* always descends a fifth, as the following example shows.

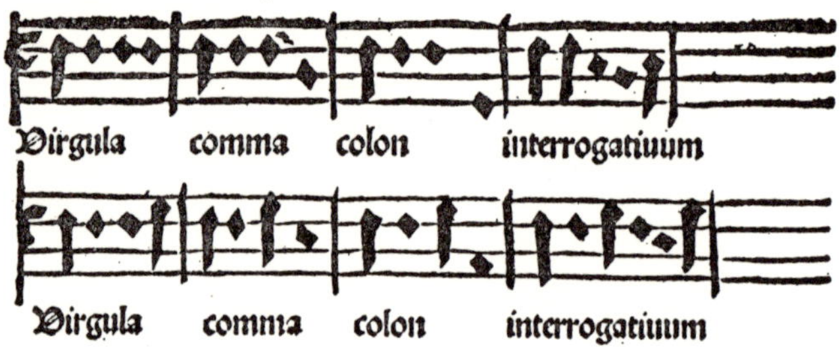

How are these punctuation marks indicated? A *virgula* is usually shown by a short lateral line, as / ; a comma by two dots, as : ; a *colon* by one dot which should then be followed by a capital letter. If the *colon* is a final it is called a period. An interrogation is shown by a dot with a curved line above, as ?.

End of the third tract; the fourth on mensural music follows.

[Letter to Willibald Pirckheimer]

To the eminent Willibald Pirckheimer, town councilor of Nürnberg, and a man truly praiseworthy in every faculty, Johannes Cochlaeus sends heartiest greetings.

Most distinguished Willibald Pirckheimer:

If one cannot repay a debt of gratitude in a fitting measure, he can at least express and extend his thankfulness. You have indeed placed me under obligation to you for the many kindnesses due to your beneficence, so that very deservedly I am forever indebted to you in a perpetual and heartfelt bond of gratitude. Therefore, although I do not have the means to reciprocate your benevolence, I am all the more disposed to express my gratitude.

For this reason I gladly offer you all my work, all my studies, vigils, and lucubrations in which I have presumed to develop a plan to advance the knowledge of our youth. Moreover, in my opinion there is nothing more advantageous and agreeable in the studies of our adolescents than compendious instruction in both grammar and music. For whatever you try to build up without grammatical instruction is bound to fall, and without musical instruction every song is lethargic (a state which affects the adolescent most particularly).

Therefore, after coming to the school of St. Lorenz on your recommendation, and later that of the Prior, I have long since dedicated to both of you the rudiments of each art, rudiments that were written down in the midst of the distractions of other duties. Since my *Grammatices Quadrivium*, recently printed here, is now daily being used with good results (thanks be to God) by our youth, it is just as necessary to have a compendium of music. This need is easily established in the minds of all who have considered either the precepts of Aristotle's *Politics* or the tender period of youth as especially suitable to this art. In addition, music here is studied at first not so much in a contemplative way (as Boethius and Giorgio Valla have left it to us) as in a practical way, in a kind of music in which our countrymen are remarkably proficient, both in playing various resonant instruments and in the pleasing sound of their voices. Moreover, our people are extremely pleased with this kind of music.

But you also, although occupied with very lofty studies, with jurisprudence and other matters, are most familiar with the pleasures of music, since you excel in the art of singing and in playing all types of wind[1] instruments, and with even greater care instruct all your children in sweet sounding harmony.[2] Accept, therefore, I pray, our *Tetrachordum* under your patronage, because it has the same purpose as the *Quadrivium* recently dedicated to you and sent to the printer. Farewell from our schools, on the eleventh of July, in the year of salvation 1511.

[1] Cochlaeus's phrase, *omnimoda instrumentorum tractandorum*, is rather ambiguous and could be interpreted in several ways.

[2] Pirckheimer had five daughters, of whom three married and two entered a convent. Langosch, *op. cit.*, p. 166, ftn. 391. In 1511 the oldest daughter was 13.

FOURTH TRACT OF COCHLAEUS'S *TETRACHORDUM*:

Principles of Mensural Music

CHAPTER 1

Mensural Music

What is mensural music? Music whose sounds are measured according to varied notes and signs. The measurement of sounds is twofold, continuous and intervallic.

What is continuous measurement? That which consists of a continuous amount of sound in relation to its duration, for a maxima has a larger measurement than a long, since its sound continues for a greater length of time.

What is intervallic measurement? Intervals or distances between sounds arranged in a proportional relationship. This has been treated earlier in relation to consonances and intervals. Now continuous measurement will be discussed.

How many kinds are there? Two, essential and accidental. What is essential measurement? Measurement given to notes and rests according to their proper value in *modus*, *tempus*, and *prolatio*.

What is accidental measurement? Measurement which gives an accidental value to notes and rests. This occurs in two ways: first, according to the accidental value of notes in alteration, imperfection, diminution, etc.; second, according to various commensurable proportions. All these things will be considered briefly, individually, and as clearly as possible.

CHAPTER 2

Notes

What is a note? It is a representation of an actual or an omitted tone. What is an actual tone? One which is indicated by notes. What is an omitted tone? One which is indicated by rests.

How many notes are essential? Five, which are maxima, long, breve, semibreve, and minim.

What is a maxima? A quadrangular note with a stem ascending or descending from the right side, as at (a).

a

What is a long? A square note with a stem ascending or descending, as at (b).

b

What is a breve? A square note without stem or flag, as at (c).

c

What is a semibreve? A note which is written in a triangular or rhomboid shape. It is triangular if a breve is divided diametrically into two parts, and rhomboid when it has four sides that are not orthogonal, that is, rectangular, as at (d).[3]

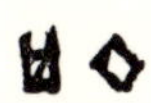
d

What is a minim? A note written like a semibreve and with a stem extending upward or downward from the tip of either angle, as at (e).

e

The essential measurement of tones (called *modus*, *tempus*, and *prolatio*) is contained in the perfection or imperfection of these five notes. All smaller notes are imperfect or binary.

How many such notes are there? Three, the semiminim, fusa, and semifusa.

What is a semiminim? A note written like a blackened minim, or as an empty note-head with a stem having a flag extending to the right, as at (f).

f

What is a fusa? A note like the semiminim and with a flag added to the stem, as at (g).

g

What is a semifusa? It is a blackened minim with two flags, or an empty one with three flags, two above and one below, as at (h). Because of its speed it is not suitable for the human voice. Rather, it is used in musical instruments when cadences are formed from the movement of a note to its closest neighbor.

h

[3] The two semibreve forms come from Gaffurius, *op. cit.*, p. 82, and are also present in Glarean, *op. cit.*, II, 225.

CHAPTER 3

Ligatures

What is a ligature? It is a collection of single notes forming specific note-shapes. How many notes are ligated? Four. Which are they? Maxima, long, breve, and semibreve. But when a maxima is ligated it does not change its value. How many rules of ligatures are there? Seven.

1. When a ligature has a stem ascending from its left side, its first and second notes are semibreves.
2. A ligature with its stem descending from its left side is a breve.
3. All middle notes are breves. For this reason it is incorrect to make a middle note a long or to put a stem on any middle note.
4. An initial note without a stem is a breve if the second note is higher.
5. An initial note without a stem is a long if the second note is lower.
6. A final square note approached from above is a long.
7. Every note with an ascending or descending stem on the right side is a long. From the preceding it is evident that a long can occur at beginning or end, not in the middle, and that a breve can occur at beginning or middle, but not at the end, unless two notes are ligated.

CHAPTER 4

Rests and Dots

What is a rest? It is a sign showing the intentional omission of a tone. It has been instituted for three reasons: first, for relief in breathing and in sound; second, because of difficulty in finding the proper note of a melody or consonance; third, for the sake of the pleasantness of a song, since the more variety and grace it possesses the more pleasing it will sound to human ears.

How many kinds of rests are there? Six,[4] namely: general, *modi*, *longa*, *pausa*, *semipausa*, *suspirium*, *semisuspirium*.

What is a general rest? It is one or two lines drawn through all staff lines to show the end of a song. Another general rest occurs when an identical rest (especially a breve or semibreve) is placed simultaneously in all parts of a contrapuntal song.

What is a *pausa modi*? It is a line of three *tempora* (equal to three breves) which reaches four staff-lines and occupies three spaces; it is worth a perfect long.

What is a *pausa longa*? It is a line which occupies two spaces and reaches three staff-lines.

What is a *pausa*? It is a line drawn from one staff-line to the next and occupying one space; it is worth a breve. It is given the general name *pausa* or rest because it is used more frequently and is equal to one complete *tempus*.

What is a *semipausa*? A line which extends down from any staff-line to the middle of a space; it is worth a semibreve.

What is a *suspirium*? A line rising from a staff-line to the middle of a space; it is worth a minim.

What is a *semisuspirium*? A line rising from a staff-line to the middle of a space and with a flag extending to the left from its tip; it is worth a semiminim. Here are examples.

[4] Cochlaeus has *sextuplex*. Although he lists seven kinds of rests, a general rest is apparently not considered a true rest. This is also the teaching of Glarean, who says that he is following Cochlaeus on this subject. See Miller, *op. cit.*, II, 227.

What is a dot? A very small mark added to a note.

How many kinds of dots are there? Three, a dot of division, perfection, and addition.

What is a dot of division? A dot put before or after a note. It does not change the value of the note, but shows whether it should be applied to and counted with a preceding or followed group to form a ternary division in the notes, as at (x).

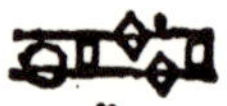

x

What is a dot of perfection? A dot which follows a perfect note to keep it perfect and prevent its becoming imperfect.

What is a dot of addition? A dot following an imperfect note and adding a half to the value of its note. Thus a dot after a maxima is worth a long, after a long it is worth a breve, and after a breve a semibreve, as at (z).

z

CHAPTER 5

Modus, Tempus, Prolatio

What is a *modus*? It is the measurement of longs in maximas and of breves in longs. It is twofold, *maior* and *minor*.

What is a *modus maior*? It is the measurement of longs in maximas.

What is a *modus minor*? It is the measurement of breves in longs.

What is *tempus*? It is the value given to breves, or the measurement of semibreves in breves.

What is *prolatio*? It is the value given to semibreves, or the measurement of minims in semibreves.

These species are all twofold, perfect and imperfect. They are perfect when the total is divided by three, and imperfect when it is divided by two. In *modus maior perfectus* there are three longs in a maxima, and in *modus minor perfectus* there are three breves in a long; in *modus maior imperfectus* there are two longs in a maxima, and in *modus minor imperfectus* there are two breves in a long.

Likewise, in *tempus perfectum* there are three semibreves in one breve, and in *tempus imperfectum* there are two semibreves in one breve. Finally, in *prolatio perfecta* there are three minims in one semibreve, and in *prolatio imperfecta* there are two minims in one semibreve, as this example shows.

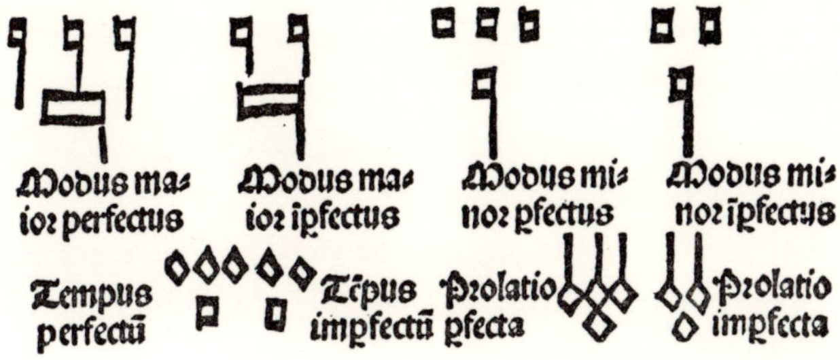

CHAPTER 6

Signs and Tactus

What is a sign? It is the primary means of recognizing *modus*, *tempus*, and *prolatio* in a song.

How many kinds of signs are there? Two, intrinsic and extrinsic. An extrinsic sign is explicit, as a circle or semicircle, An intrinsic sign is implicit, as the blackening of notes and the arrangements of rests.

Thus, more recent musicians ascribe a circle without a number to *tempus perfectum*, and a semicircle to *tempus imperfectum*. But if a number is added to a circle, the circle indicates *modus* and the number *tempus*. If a dot is written in a circle that does not have a number, the circle shows *tempus* and the dot *prolatio*, as seen in this diagram.

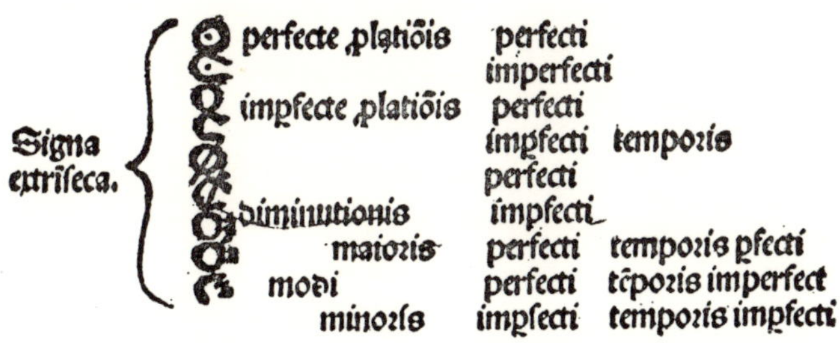

Intrinsic signs can be recognized through three rules.
1. If three longs are blackened, or if a rest occupies three spaces, the song belongs to *modus perfectus*. (We do not speak any longer about *modus maior*, since it is not used because of the excessive slowness of its notes, for a maxima would equal nine perfect *tempora*). An unblackened long is perfect, for if it were originally imperfect, it would be meaningless to blacken it, as at (m).

m 

2. If three blackened breves or their equivalents, or two identically placed semibreve rests are found in a song, they indicate *tempus perfectum*, as at (n).

n 

3. If three semibreves are blackened, or two *suspiria* rests are placed together, they show *prolatio perfecta*, which is commonly called *maior*, as at (o).

o 

Moreover, absence of numbers indicates *modus imperfectus*, and absence of a dot in a circle shows *prolatio imperfecta*. An incomplete circle indicates *tempus imperfectum*. But the sign for *tempus imperfectum* should not be an exact half-circle, but two-thirds of a circle, since only one-third of a breve's value is removed in *tempus imperfectum*. For such a breve contains two semibreves, not one and one-half, which would be half of a perfect breve.

How many extrinsic signs are there that are additional and not primary? Seven. What are they? Signs of *reinceptio* (repetition), *convenientia* (accord), *pausandus* (holding), soft *b*, hard ♮, *F fa ut*, and *c sol fa ut*, as seen in this example.

What is mensural *tactus*? It is a continuous movement maintained in a given measurement, for time is recognized by movement, and also the temporal duration of a tone. A semibreve in any time signature can be measured by a mensural *tactus*, except in proportions and augmentation. The tactus of individual notes in any time signature can be seen very easily in this quadrate example.

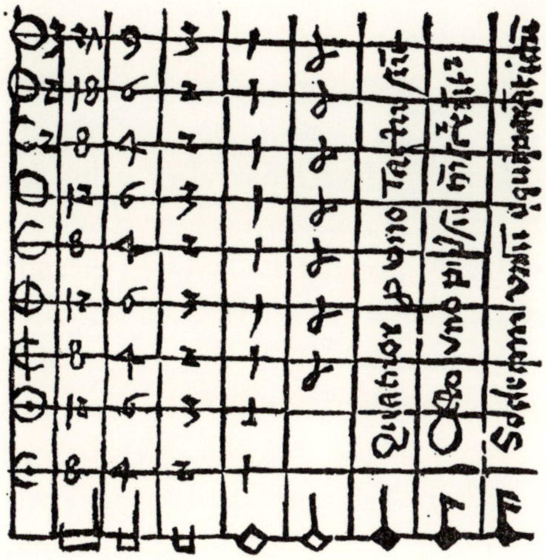

In the relationship of note-values one can also observe how many *tactus* are contained in any note of any time signature. To show this more readily an example in *modus perfectus* is given.

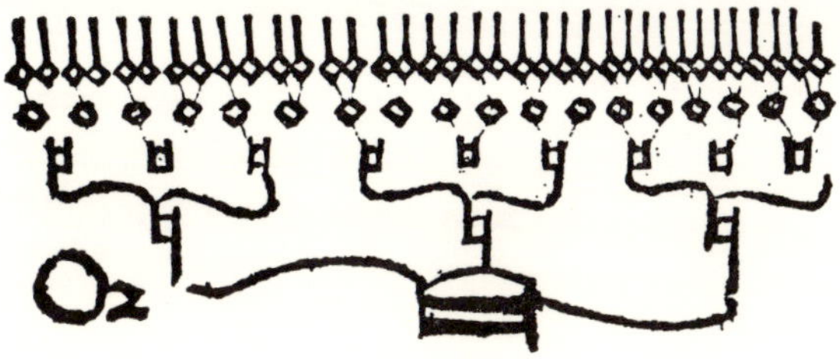

CHAPTER 7

Augmentation and Diminution

What is augmentation? It is the mental lengthening of note values. It occurs in *prolatio perfecta* when one minim is measured by a complete *tactus*, and a perfect semibreve by three *tactus*.

What is its extrinsic sign? A circle or semicircle with an inscribed dot, provided that they are found in just one voice-part of a song, as at (t). If they are found in all parts of a song there is no augmentation, but simply *prolatio perfecta*, in which three minims are counted in one *tactus*.

What is the extrinsic sign of augmentation? Paucity of notes which lack a sign of repetition and which are placed in only one voice-part of a song.

What is diminution? It is the removal of value from the measurement of notes. It occurs in *tempus perfectum* when a complete circle is divided by a line, as at (p). In diminution the number of notes is not lessened (for the *perfectum* signature is retained), but a third part of the measurement is removed. So the *tactus* is faster than if the circle were not intersected by the line, although both the value of the notes and their ternary perfection remain unchanged. But since duple proportion is easier, diminution occurs most often in duple measurement.

p

In addition, in these signs at (q) there is a diminution of *tempus perfectum* if they occur equally in all parts of a song, for a perfect breve or three semibreves are counted in one *tactus*. This is usually called *proportio tripla*, because three notes move in one *tactus*.

q

What is *semiditas*? It is the removal of half the temporal value of the measurement, and occurs only in *tempus imperfectum*, as at (r) or (s). For thus two semibreves equal a single *tactus* in one voice-part of a song, while one semibreve equals a tactus in another part which is not diminished by a line dividing the signature or by a number added to it. Augmentation and diminution can be shown in two other ways: first, by a canonic inscription, as, "let a breve be a long", and the reverse; second, by a larger proportion opposed to one smaller, or the reverse.

r

s

CHAPTER 8

Imperfection of Notes

What is imperfection? It is the removal of temporal value of a perfect note in a ternary relationship. It occurs only in perfect signatures, for a note in imperfect mensuration is not made imperfect but is imperfect already.

How many kinds of imperfection are there? Two, total and partial. What is total imperfection? Removal of exactly one-third of a note's value, as a long imperfected by a semibreve in *tempus perfectum* and within a breve ratio, or a breve imperfected by a minim in *prolatio perfecta* and within a semibreve ratio. Parts of notes include *propinqua*, *remota*, *remotior*, and *remotissima*, as can be seen in the preceding diagram of the relationship of note-values.

One of the notes, a minim, is only imperfect, and another a maxima, is only imperfected. Some notes of diverse properties can imperfect and be imperfected, as a long, breve, and semibreve. For example, a breve imperfects a long in *modus perfectus*, but is imperfected by a semibreve in *tempus perfectum*.

How many rules of imperfection are there? Six.

1. In *modus perfectus* a long is imperfected by a breve, or its rest, or an equivalent value, when one of these immediately follows the long, unless a *punctus perfectionis* or *divisionis* intervenes.
2. In *tempus perfectum* a breve is imperfected by a semibreve immediately following it, or by a semibreve rest, or by smaller notes equivalent to a semibreve. But a breve remains perfect if it is followed by another breve, or a breve rest, or two semibreve rests, or if followed by a *punctus perfectionis*.
3. In *prolatio perfecta* a semibreve is imperfected by a minim, a minim rest, or two semiminims. It remains perfect if it precedes another semibreve, a semibreve rest, or two minim rests.
4. Color or blackening of perfect notes makes them imperfect by removing a third of their value.
5. A rest is not imperfected or altered. A note is not imperfected by another of the same kind following it or preceding it; therefore, a larger note is always imperfected by a smaller note.
6. A larger note can be imperfected *a parte remota ante et post* in the ratio of a *pars propinqua perfecta ad totum*, as a long imperfected by two semibreves, and a breve by two minims.

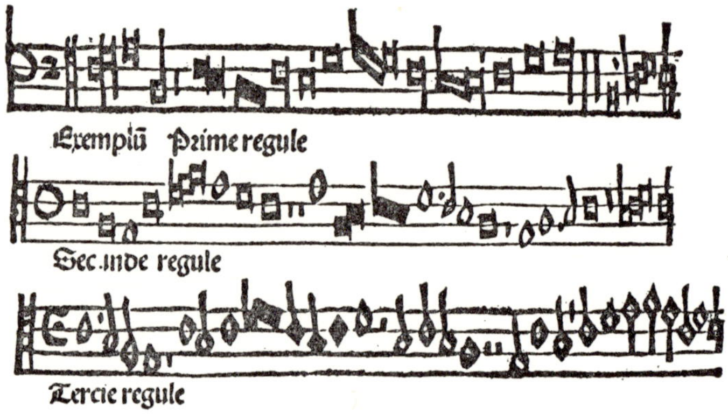

CHAPTER 9

Alteration and Syncopation

What is alteration? It is doubling the value of a note. It occurs only in *tempus perfectum* (just as does imperfection), to complete a ternary grouping. But it is different than imperfection, in which one part is superabundant and is therefore removed from the whole.

In alteration one part is lacking to form a ternary group. The second note is always altered, not the first. If you doubled the first note you would make an imperfect whole rather than an altered part. But if you double the second note, the first note is counted with it in a ternary group, which is the reason for alteration. The second note could not assume the note-shape of the total ternary value, like the first note, because another total ternary value would follow it and thus it could not be imperfected. But if the first note had the note-shape of the total ternary value, it could easily be imperfected by the second note, and thus an alteration would be meaningless.

How many rules of alteration are there? Four.

1. In *modus perfectus* the second breve is altered when two breves remain which are not included in a ternary group.
2. In *tempus perfectum* a semibreve is altered when two semibreves are superabundant, which occurs most frequently in a ligature of two semibreves with a following [breve].
3. In *prolatio perfecta* a minim is altered when two minims exceed a ternary grouping.

4. Alteration is distinguished most clearly from imperfection by a *punctis divisionis*, for the alteration of middle notes or the imperfection of outer notes is shown by the placement of the dot.

What is syncopation? It is the repetition, after a larger note-value, of a note-value counted equally with the same preceding note-value. It occurs when it is placed with many larger note-values, so that a few smaller note-values have between them larger note-values which sound against the *tactus*.

How many rules of syncopation are there? Two.

1. A minim should not recur after a breve rest and rarely after a semibreve rest.
2. A semibreve should not recur after a long rest and rarely after a breve rest.

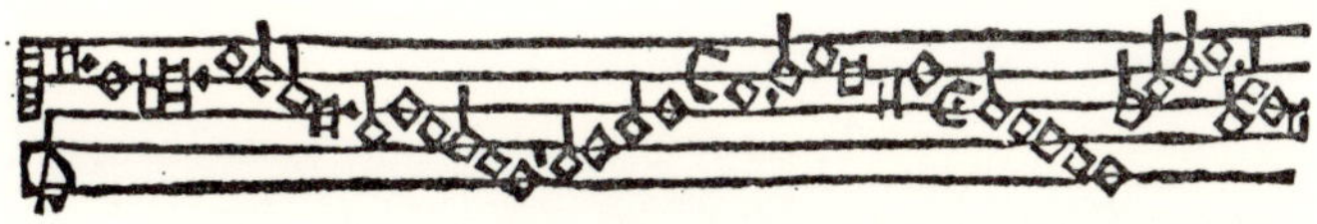

CHAPTER 10

Proportions

What is proportion? It is the mutual relation of two quantities (of any kind) that belong to the same genus. It occurs principally in numbers, secondly in consonances, and thirdly in note-values.

Proportions are divided into equal proportions, as four to four, and unequal proportions which are greater, as four to two, and lesser, as two to four. The five genera of greater inequality are as follows: *multiplex*, in which the larger number includes the smaller many times exactly (two, three, or four times), as 4 to 2; *superparticulare*, in which the larger number includes the smaller once and one aliquot part, as 3 to 2; *superpartiens*, in which the larger number includes the smaller once and one aliquant part, as 5 to 3; *multiplex superparticulare*, in which the larger number includes the smaller many times and one aliquot part, as 5 to 2; *multiplex superpartiens*, in which the larger number includes the smaller many times and one aliquant part, as 8 to 3. There are also five genera of lesser equality having the same names prefixed with the preposition *sub*.

What is an aliquot part? A part taken several times which equals its total exactly, as two taken twice equals four, and taken three times equals six.

What is an aliquant part? A part which consists of several aliquot parts. When it is taken several times it does not equal the total exactly, but is either more or less, as three to five or three to eight.

There are infinite species of individual genera, just as there are of numbers, but in songs we very rarely use more than *multiplex* and *superparticulare* genera, e.g., in *multiplex* such species as *dupla*, *tripla*, and *quadrupla*, and in *superparticulare*, the *sesquialtera* and *sesquitertia* species. Because of their difficulty the others are very rarely applied to musical notes.

How many rules should be observed in writing proportions? Three.
1. A proportion is not written correctly unless it has two numbers, because the same number has different meanings in different proportions, as 3 to 2, or *sesquialtera*, 3 to 1, or *tripla*, and 3 to 4, or *subsesquitertia*.
2. A proportion should be related to a single mensuration sign, for if diverse voice-parts of a song have diverse mensuration signs, a proportion will not be written correctly in relation to the number of notes; for example, three breves of *tempus perfectum* against two breves of *tempus imperfectum* will not form *sesquialtera*, or 3 to 2, but *sesquiquarta*, or 9 to 4, since three perfect breves contain nine semibreves, and two imperfect breves contain only four semibreves.
3. A proportion is removed in two ways, either by writing the opposite proportion or by interposing a mensuration sign. The easiest proportion is *dupla*, since it is easy to recognize the half of the proportion. Therefore, this proportion is more common and in greater use than the others.

What is *proportio dupla*? A larger number containing a smaller exactly twice. In songs, two notes are counted against one of the same kind in a proportion written $\frac{2}{1}$, or $\frac{4}{2}$, or in similar numbers.

Ex. 4

What is *proportio tripla*? A larger number of notes related to a smaller number and containing the smaller number exactly three times. The proportion is written as $\frac{3}{1}$ or $\frac{6}{2}$, or in a similar way.

Ex. 5

What is *quadrupla*? A larger number of notes related to a smaller number and containing the smaller number exactly four times. Quadrupla is written as $\frac{4}{1}$, or $\frac{8}{2}$, or with other numbers.

Ex. 6

What is *sesquialtera*? A larger number of notes related to a smaller number and containing the smaller number one and one-half times. The proportion is written as $\frac{3}{2}$, or $\frac{6}{4}$, or in a similar way.

Ex. 7

What is *sesquitertia proportio*? A larger number of notes related to a smaller number and containing the smaller number one and one-third times. The proportion is written $\frac{4}{3}$, or in a similar way. But other species of proportions are not discussed in this rather brief compendium because of their rarity and their difficulty in singing.

Proportions which form consonances have been treated earlier in a general way. They are discussed in greater detail in the tract on counterpoint that we published in Cologne.[5] From the latter it is useful to include here as a corollary some rules of counterpoint.

1. Counterpoint should begin with perfect consonances. But this is arbitrary, since it often begins with imperfect consonances, as here:

Ex. 8

2. Two perfect consonances of the same species cannot move in ascending or descending parallel motion in a song, as at (a).[6] This rule is not arbitrary but legal, rejecting any exception.

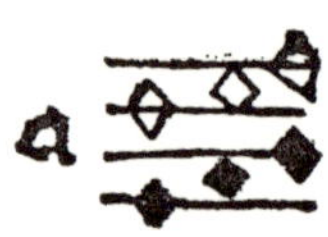

[5] *Musica* (1507), f. 23ʳ.

[6] Examples (a), (b), and (c) are lacking in the 1511 edition, and have been included here by using the corresponding examples in *Musica* of 1507.

3. Two similar perfect consonances can follow each other immediately if they move in dissimilar and contrary motion, as at (b).

4. Several stationary and perfect consonances of the same species can be written in a song, as at (c).

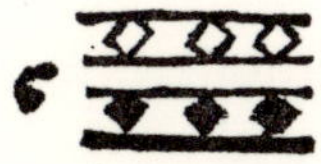

5. Several similar perfect consonances cannot follow each other in ascending or descending parallel motion if only a minim or minim rest is interposed, for they seem to move in immediate parallel motion because of the very short duration of a minim rest or of a minim note, as this example shows.

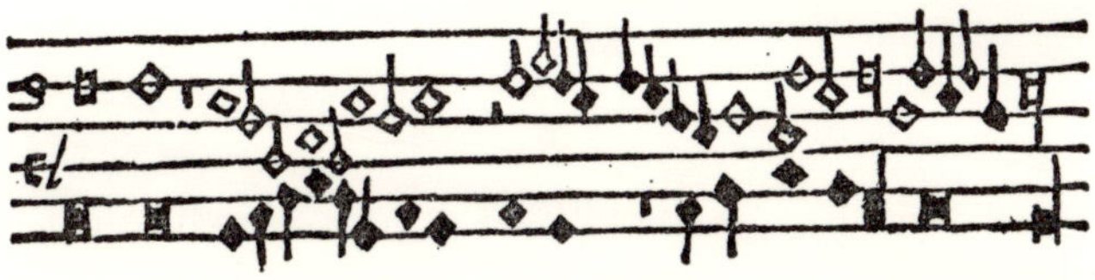

Some also do not allow similar perfect consonances in ascending or descending motion if a semibreve rest in interposed, although many disagree with this.[7] For this reason a dissonance is infrequently allowed between similar perfect consonances.

6. Many perfect and dissimilar consonances can move in ascending or descending motion, as a unison to a fifth, a fifth to an octave, an octave to a fifth, and so on, as at (d).

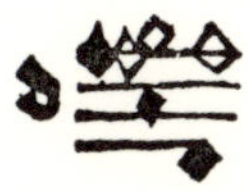

7. Between two similar perfect consonances there should be at least one imperfect consonance, as at (e).

[7] On f.26v of the 1511 edition, the first line of text is lacking, and has been adduced from *Musica*.

8. Between two perfect consonances it is fitting to place several similar or dissimilar imperfect consonances, as one, two, three, or four thirds, and one or more tenths. The following is an example.

9. Several ascending parallel sixths can rarely or never be used in note-against-note counterpoint, although many descending sixths can be written if the last sixth is followed by the octave it requires, as at (f).

f 

10. Sometimes a tenth can follow a sixth if the tenor descends a third or fourth. A third can also follow a sixth if the tenor ascends a fourth, as at (g).

g

11. In a discant, resolution to the closest consonant should be sought, as when discant and tenor on a soft third move in contrary motion to a unison, as at (h).

 h

But from a hard third they move in contrary motion to a fifth, as at (i).

 i

12. When a discant a third above a tenor rises one step, the tenor descends a fifth, so that together they form an octave. Also, when a tenor an octave below a discant rises a fifth, the discant descends one step, so that the octave moves very nicely to a third, as at (k).

 k

13. When tenor and discant are a major sixth apart, both move in contrary motion to an octave which is next to the sixth. But a minor sixth more frequently moves in oblique motion to a fifth, so that one voice-part of the song is stationary, as at (l). The interval can also move in contrary motion to an octave.

14. Every song should end on a perfect consonance, either the unison (as is customary in Venice), the octave, or the fifteenth. Every school of music commonly observes this in order to end with a perfect harmonic mean, for it is the end that is perfect (according to the philosopher [Aristotle]).

Since the end has now been mentioned, it is fitting to add from the same tract some rules and examples concerning the endings of songs, and first four rules on composition in three parts.

1. In cadences (*clausulae*), the discant rises from a sixth with the tenor to an octave with it; the bass, a fifth below the tenor, either drops to an octave with it, or ascends to a unison, or to a fifth above the tenor.

2. If the tenor ends on *mi*, the discant and tenor still move from a sixth to an octave, but the bass, a third below the tenor, ends on a fifth below it with the syllables *sol re*.

3. If the tenor uses the discant's melodic pattern,[8] the discant can be placed a third above, and end on a unison with the tenor or a third above it; the bass, a third below the tenor, will close on the lower octave.

4. If the tenor again uses the discant's melodic pattern, the latter may move from a penultimate fifth above the tenor to end on a third above it. The bass, a sixth below the tenor, should meet it on the octave and thus move in tenths with the discant, as these examples show:

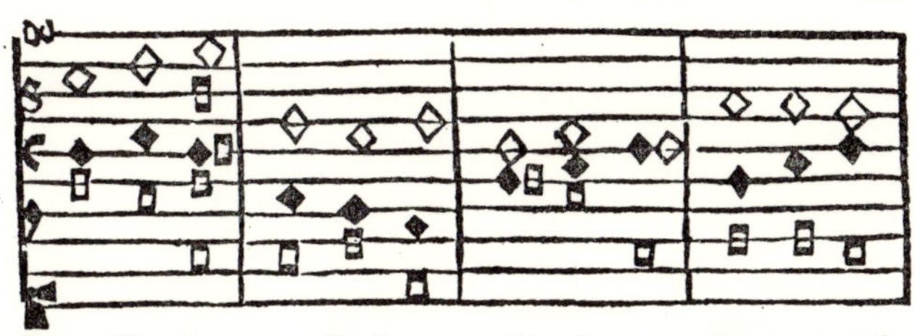

Exemplū prime Scđe Tercie Quarte regule

[8] *i.e.*, the notes *a*, *b*, *c*, as shown in the first example of these four rules.

But when a place is given to a fourth voice (commonly called alto), five rules are followed.

1. In the first cadence, the alto in the penultimate chord will be a fourth above the tenor and a fifth above it on the final. The bass makes the fourth a concord because it is a fifth below the tenor.
2. In the second cadence, the alto in the penultimate chord is a third above the tenor and a fourth above it in the final. In the penultimate chord it is a fifth above the bass and an octave above in the final.
3. In the third cadence, the alto can be a third above the tenor. In this case it will be a fifth above the bass on the penultimate chord and a tenth above it on the final. It can also be an octave above the bass on the penultimate and a twelfth above it on the final.
4. In the fourth cadence, the alto, a fourth below the tenor, rises with it, but stays a third above the bass on the penultimate chord and a fifth above it on the final.
5. If the alto takes the discant's melodic pattern, the bass, a sixth below the alto on the penultimate chord, will move to an octave below it. The tenor, taking the place of the alto,[9] has a third above the bass on the penultimate chord and a fifth above it on the final, as these examples show:

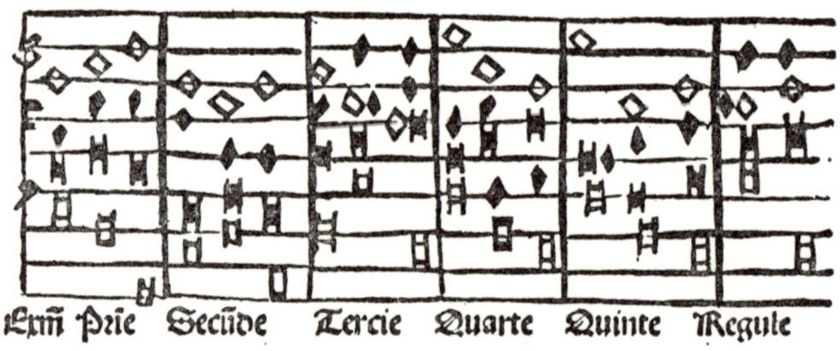

Moreover, very useful examples can be presented here which truly offer a great deal to a teacher's art and enjoyment. For what is used more frequently in a choir than the singing of psalms? What is sweeter, more pleasant, more elegant, than the lyric harmony of odes? What is easier to understand than such harmonies? For this reason we decided to add to our compendium some four-part harmonies (*Tetraphoni*) in a recent style of composition, since they can be of great use both for practice and for pleasure. We have composed

[9] In exx. 4 and 5 the alto and tenor invert their cadence notes.

them with effort and haste[10] in five Tones and certain poetic meters.

Therefore, these suggestions are written for the sake of the harmonious blending of the individual parts which consist of only a few notes.

1. A text should be set according to the tenor, for verses have an unequal number of syllables; thus one verse needs more notes than another, and their number should be determined by the chorale melody.

2. The rise and fall of the tenor melody should be watched especially at the middle and end of a verse, for all voices do not rise and fall at the same time. Thus, according to the number of notes at these places, the other parts should harmonize with the tenor's rising or falling note.

3. The value of notes can be varied easily, both because some words are correctly sung with longs, some with breves, and because they are more pleasing in their variety, especially in music. In the same way a variation of note values is allowed in *tactus planus* and in triple measurement.

4. In *tactus planus* the penultimate note should be prolonged with a certain solemnity, so that a full consonance strikes the ears and the song quietly subsides and comes to rest on the final.

5. When you set the notes be sure to write the text first, then the notes, which will be in mensural rather than choral notation, if you really want to vary the measurement. In this way you can immediately determine the notes, and (whenever it is appropriate), you can sing them very easily in consonant harmony in the choir.

Four-part psalmody in Tones follows.

Ex. 9 **Tone 1**

[10] This phrase, *tumultario sane stilo elucubravimus*, seems to imply that Cochlaeus was compelled to compose his four-part settings hurriedly and when he had free time, probably because of the press of his regular duties. This complaint about the pressure of other activities occurs in several places in the *Tetrachordum*.

Tone 2

Tone 3

Tone 4

Tone 5

It remains now that we present in four-part counterpoint those metric genera that are most used. From them a youth may learn about the melodious blending of words, the diverse arrangement of metric feet, and likewise the various poetic genera. But here we have touched upon only a few metric genera, since they have been treated more fully in my *Quadrivium Grammatices*.[11]

It is not my plan to teach the poetic meters here. Besides, other occupations often hinder our work a great deal, often hold it up, often completely overwhelm it. So it is enough to combine four poetic genera with musical settings, for if we pursued all of them we would waste time and weary the reader.

But it is pleasant to join poetry and music, and to recreate a conception of antiquity. For who does not know that *carmina* are delivered by singing (*canendo*), as if *canimina*? How? Did not lyric poems join their words to the sound of the lyre? What about Phemius in Homer and Ioppas in Vergil? Did not they apply harmonious strains to the most distinguished heroic poems? Therefore, it is with good reason that we present these metrical compositions. But we have not observed the metric feet in every place, favoring the melodies rather than the meters.

Ex. 10 Elegiac Song

[11] Published in Nürnberg in 1511.

Examples from Ovid

Forma bonum fragile est, quantumque accedit ad annos
Fit minor, et spatio carpitur ipsa suo.[12]
Et tibi iam venient cani, formose, capilli,
Iam venient ruge, que tibi corpus arent.[13]
Vina parant animos faciuntque caloribus aptos:
Cura fugit multo diluiturque mero.
Tunc veniunt risus, tum pauper cornua sumit,
Tunc dolor et cure rugaque frontis abit.[14]
Conscia mens recti fama mendacia ridet,
Sed nos in vicium credula turba sumus.[15]
Scilicet ut fulvum spectatur in ignibus aurum,
Tempore sic duro est inspicienda fides.[16]
Donec eris felix, multos numerabis amicos:
Tempora si fuerint nubila, solus eris.[17]

To these poems I hope it is permissible to add some others less perfect, so to speak, that we sing daily in our new school.

Mane tuum petimus numen, o spiritus alme:
Sensibus a nostris nubila crassa fuge,
Pectora nostra sacro perfunde liquore Heliconis,
Ut fontes nostros docta Thalia colat
Mentibus o nostris illabere, redde furorem
Divinum, vates quo calvere sacri.

Ex. 11 Iambic Song

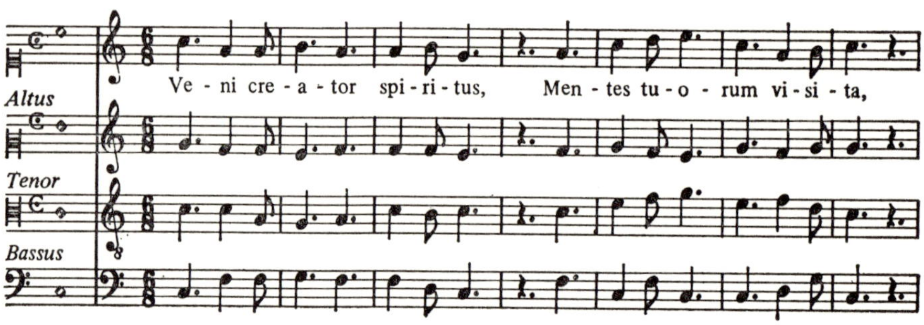

[12] *Ars Amatoria*, II, 113.
[13] *Ibid.*, II, 117.
[14] *Ibid.*, I, 237.
[15] *Fasti*, IV, 311.
[16] *Tristia*, I, 5, 25.
[17] *Ibid.*, I, 9, 5.

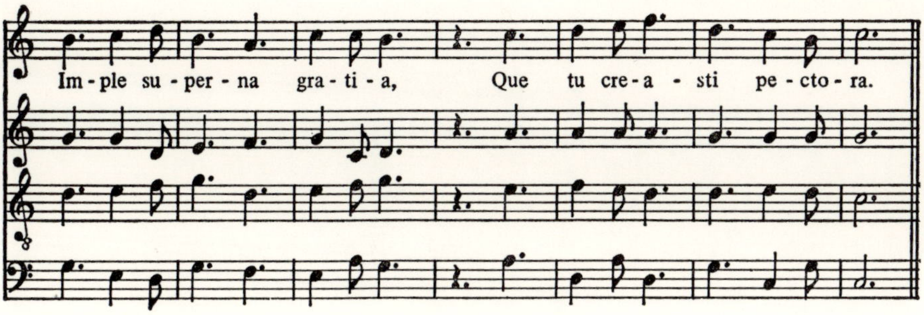

Conditor alme siderum, Eterna lux credentium
Christe redemptor omnium, Exaudi preces supplicum.[18]
Veni redemptor gentium, Ostende partum virginis,
Miretur omne seculum, Talis decet partus deum.[19]
A solis ortus cardine, Ad usque terrae limitem,
Christum canamus principem, Natum Maria virgine.[20]
Hostis Herodes impie, Christum venire quid times,
Non arripit mortalia, Qui regna dat celestia.[21]

These meters are iambic dimeters, which are most frequent in hymns. But I could not find this genus in Horace or Boethius.
Horace has one iambic trimeter in his Epodes[22] and Boethius has more, likewise trimeters.

Ex. 12

Sapphic Song

[18] *AM* 182.
[19] *H* 80, *passim.*
[20] *LU* 400
[21] *AM* 288.
[22] *Epode* 17.

Martyris Christi colimus triumphum,
Annuum tempus venerando cuius,
Cernua vocis prece iam rotundus,
Orbis adorat.[23]
Phoebe sylvarumque potens Diana,
Lucidum celi decus, o colendi,
Semper et culti, date quae precamur,
Tempore sacro.[24]
Iste confessor Domini sacratus,
Festa plebs cuius celebret per orbem,
Hodie letus meruit secreta,
Scandere celi.[25]

In addition to these sacred texts may it be permissible to add a poem that was written with hasty pen and insufficient reflection, in the midst of the distractions of other duties. It does not aspire so much to elegance as to arousing heartfelt devotion. We are accustomed to sing it in the afternoon in our schools.

[Hymn to St. Catherine]

Diva nunc nobis Catharina adesto,
Ut pios vates Sophiamque castam
Mente discamus memori, reclude
Pectora dura.
Dividum nobis Heliconis amnem,

[23] *H*, p. 298, *passim*.
[24] Horace, *Carmen Saeculare*, 1.
[25] *AM* 656.

Porrigat sponsus tuus, ut nitorem
Lingua perdiscat latii, vetusti
Grammata culta.
Spiritus sancti veneranda virgo:
Celici felix tripodis Sybilla,
Perfer ad nostros animos sacratas,
Numinis auras.

Ex. 13 Choriambic Song

Two examples by Horace follow.

Scriberis Vario fortis et hostium
Victor Meonii carminis alite,
Quam rem cumque ferox navibus aut equis
Miles te duce gesserit.[26]
Heu, heu, quantus equis, quantus adest viris
Sudor! quanta moves funera Dardane
Genti! iam galeam Pallas et Aegida
Currusque et rabiem parat.[27]

A Scholastic Poem

Audi virgo parens angelicum chere!
Salve grata Deo, Rector olympicus
Est tecum, superas femineum genus
Fructu candida celico.
Nunc vatum resonat dulce melos chorus,
En virgo peperit candida filium
Mundi certa salus, te Dominam colunt
Tellus styx polus equora.
Fontis Pierii rore salubriter
Vatum labra rigas qui tua numina
Poscunt corde pio, nos famulos tuos
Sanctas instrue litteras.

Hexastich of Johannes Cochlaeus to the reader.

Quisquis amat musas cui carmina dulcia cure,
Hunc natura trahit, mens regit, ornat honos,
Vates ac sapiens idem, qui musicus olim
Dulcisono gaudent nunc quoque templa melo,
Quare hos chara modos cape leta fronte inventus,
Quos labor excudit, quos pius edit amor.

End of *Tetrachordum Musices*, published at Nürnberg in the printing office of the Rev. Fr. Johannes Weyssenburger, in the year 1511.

[26] *Carmina* I, 6.

[27] *Ibid.*, I, 15, 9. After this ode Cochlaeus inserts the following: Musical notes are missing in the preceding song, for the fourth note (a semibreve) in the third phrase should be divided into two minims, so that the phrase begins with a spondee and follows with a choriamb.

Epigram of Willibald Pirckheimer to Johannes Cochlaeus

To you, Cochlaeus, wise Minerva has given natural talent, Venus a fondness for music, and handsome Apollo the lyre, but Mercury also as well as the Thespian choir have proffered facility in harmony and variety in melody. What wonder is it then, if you surpass all others in the art of music, when such deities favor your undertakings.

Chelidonius Musophilus to the reader

Delius, high-priest of the Muses, intones a varied and sweet sounding song on Olympus, and by the sea the Sirens harmoniously sing enticing melodies. The air listens to birds with their joyous songs in vocal harmony. Orpheus, and Linus too, play their music in Elysium; Cochlaeus, companion of the Muses, assists music with his art, teaching and creating poetic song.

[Glarean's poem to Johannes Cochlaeus]

To Johannes Cochlaeus of Bavaria, a panegyric poem in praise of music and David's cithara, by the Swiss Heinrich Glarean, philosopher of Cologne.

With tuneful cithara I took delight in pleasant song, and in playing the harmonious strings of a melodious lyre, which raises its graceful head with curved horns, like those you see on tame goats at play. And with ivory plectrum a plaintive string is played, while a thousand enticing tones are concealed in the swelling body.

I wonder at its tones and the smooth consonance of its harmony, how it makes concords of high, low, and median sounds. When you strike low strings it brings forth deep, sonorous tones, and with high strings it answers in soft, high tones. Finally, it is a symphony of strings that would appease even your jaws, O savage Cerberus.

But am I keeping you silent, O David, sacred and divine poet, with your venerable burden, the plaintive lyre? Your gifts are greater than Dalmatian gold and better than your hearths, O indolent Sabaean. It is related that Orpheus lured lions with a cithara and moved rocks with his tortoise-shell lyre. You also, Pluto, in your dark abode, his divine lyre has appeased, moving you to relinquish Euridice.

O most delightful Arion, by whose lyre playing sea monsters were charmed, how may I celebrate you in verse? And also Thamyras, who competed with the muses, and Marsya with Phoebus, and sounds that compete in turn with numbers? O what sweet music that recalls pleasing Iopas, and with Terpander the Timothean lyre. Strains in praise of the Dircean seer are never lacking in the shrill lyres of the centaur Chiron.

This divine gift, this venerable present, given to us from celestial realms, you also, Phoebus, have granted us. I am convinced that the cithara has come down from heaven, since I think nothing is more beautiful than its music. I, Glarean, have sung my song.

Hexastich of Johannes Cochlaeus to the reader

Everyone who delights in the arts of the muses, and who has concern for harmonious song, is supported by nature, guided by discernment, and rewarded by honor. Just as in former times poets and wise men were musicians, so also today they rejoice in churches with sweet sounding melody. Therefore, dear youth, accept these books with cheerful countenance, books written with labor and published with loving care.

APPENDIX II

Sources of *Tetrachordum Musices*

Abbreviations:

Et = *Etymologiarum* by Isadore of Seville
Ge = Jean Gerson, *De canticorum originali ratione*
Je = Jerome (pseudo-Jerome letter to Dardanus)
Mu = *Musica* by Adam von Fulda, in Gerbert III
Op = *Opus Aureum* by Wollick (I, II) and Schanppecher (III, IV)
Pr = *Practica Musicae* by Gaffurius. Page numbers refer to my edition of this treatise.
Ra = *Rationale divinorum officiorum* by Durandus
Ri = Richard of St. Victor, *Excerptionum Allegoricarum Libri*

Book	Chapter	Source(s)	Remarks
I	1		
	2	*Op* A v[r] ; *Mu* 333; Ri I, 10	
	3	*Op* A iv[r]	
	4	*Op* H ii[r]	Diagram based on *Op* Hii[v]
	5		
	6	*Et* III, cap. 20; *Pr* III, 1, p. 127	
	7	*Op* D i ff.	
	8		
	9	*Et* III, cap. 21, 22; Je; Ge, I	
	10	*Et* III, cap. 22; Je; Ge, I	

Book	Chapter	Source(s)	Remarks
II	1		
	2		
	3	*Op* B ii^r	Diagram of gamut follows *Mu* 345; *Op* B iv^r
	4	*Pr* I, 3, p. 29	
	5		
	6	*Et* III, 20; *Pr* I, 3, p. 29ff	
	7	*Mu* 345f; *Op*. B ii^r ff	Musical example identical with *Op* B iv^r
	8	*Mu* 345; *Pr* I, 4, p. 36; *Op* C ii^r	
	9	*Op* C iv^r	Exx. 1, 2, 3, are identical with *Op* C iv^v
	10	*Op* B iii	
III	1	*Op* D iii^v	
	2		
	3		
	4	*Op* E ii^r	Exx. of Tones are a condensation of *Op* E ii^r ff.
	5	*Op* E iii^r	Exx. of *differentiae* follow *Op* E iv^v ff.
	6	*Op* E iii^r	Tones for Magnificat and Benedictus follow *Op* E iii^v ff.
	7	*Ra* IV, 5	
	8		
	9	*Ra* IV, 19, 22; V, 2	
	10		
IV	1		
	2	*Op* F iv^r ; *Pr* II, 3, p. 74	
	3	*Op* G ii^v ; *Pr* II, 5, p. 78	
	4	*Op* G ii^v ; *Pr* II, 6, p. 81	
	5	*Pr* II, 7, p. 83	
	6	*Mu* 361f; *Op* F vi^v	Square diagram of mensurations is based on *Op* G i^v
	7		
	8	*Pr* II, 11, p. 92	
	9	*Pr* II, 13, p. 108; II, 15, p. 113	
	10	*Pr* III, 3, p. 124ff.; IV, 1, p. 153; *Op* H ii^r ff.	Ex. 8 is identical with *Pr* III, 3, p. 124

APPENDIX III

Opus Aureum – fol. B iv^{v}

Prime re- gule Secunde re- gule Tercie re- gule exēpla.

Caueat postremo cantilenarum compositor in speciebus perfectis et in quarta mi cōtra fa disponere: hec enim vocum congeries insuauiter aures offendit. hīc ab ipsis contrapuncti elementis seiungitur.

¶ Finis contrapuncti simplicis

Prime proprietatis bduralis Tritura prima

Prime naturalis Tritura scđa

Prime bmollaris Tritura tercia

Secūda bduralis Tritura quarta

Euouae
Ecce nomē dñi
Tecū pncipiū
pma dña
Mulieres
scda dña
Ecce ego
.3a dña
Uolo pater
Quarta dña
Lazarus
Dñe vt videā
Nisi tu dñe
Inclinauit
qnta dña
Estote fortes in bello
Salue
Seqt intonatio psalmoꝝ minoꝝ in paus pductis
Laudate pueri dñm. laudate nomē dñi.
Sz in pausis corruptis talis est forma
Deus in noie tuo saluū me fac. ꝛ in iusticia tua libera me
Intonatio psalmoꝝ maioꝝ.
Magnificat anima mea dominū

Opus Aureum – fol. E ii^r

Allgemeine Deutsche Biographie, 56 vols. Leipzig, 1875-1910.
Antiphonale monasticum pro diurnis horis. Tournai, 1934.
Appelbaum, Stanley, ed. *The Triumph of Maximilian I*. New York, 1964.
Augustine, St. "De Musica", in Migne, *PL* XXXII.
Bacchius. "Introductorio Artis Musicae", in Meibom, *Antiquae Musicae Auctores Septem*. Amsterdam, 1652.
Baines, Anthony. *Musical Instruments Through the Ages*. London, 1961.
Blaise, Albert. *Dictionnaire Latin-Français des Auteurs Chrétiens*. Strasbourg, 1954.
Boethius. "De Musica", in Migne, *PL* LXIII.
Catholic Encyclopedia, 17 vols. New York, 1907-22.
Cochlaeus, Johannes. *Musica*. Anon. treatise in the Vienna Nationalbibliothek.
— *Musica*. Cologne, 1507.
— *Tetrachordum Musices*. Nürnberg, 1511.
Du Cange, C. *Glossarium Mediae et Infimae Latinitatis*. Paris, 1840-50.
Durandus, Gulielmus. *Rationale divinorum officiorum* (1286). References are to the Venetian edition of 1568.
Fellerer, K. "Regeln des Choralvortrags aus dem 16. Jahrhundert", in *KJ* 34, 1950.
Fritsche, Otto. *Glarean*. Frauenfeld, 1890.
Gerbert, Martin. *Scriptores ecclesiastici de musica*, 3 vols., 1784.
Gerson, Jean. "De canticorum originali ratione", in *Libri et Tractatus*... Cologne, 1483.
Grove's Dictionary of Music and Musicians, 5th ed. New York, 1954.
Horace. *Carmen Saeculare*.
— *Epodes*.
Hüschen, Heinrich. "Cochlaeus", in *MGG* II.
Hugo of St. Victor. "Eruditionis didascaliae libri VII", in Migne, *PL* CLXXVI.
Isadore, St. "Etymologiarum", in Migne, *PL* LXXXII.
Jerome, St. (Pseudo-Jerome) "Epistola ad Dardanum", in Migne, *PL* IX.
Langosch, Karl. *Johannes Cochlaeus, Brevis Germaniae Descriptio*. Darmstadt, 1960.
Liber Usualis. Tournai, 1947.
Liliencron, R. von. "Die Horazischen Metren in deutschen Kompositionen des 16. Jahrhunderts", in *VfMw* III, 1887.
Mantuani, J. "Ein unbekanntes Druckwerk", in *Mitteilungen des österreichischen Verein für Bibliothekswesen* VI, 1902.
Marchettus of Padua. "Lucidarium", in Gerbert, *Scriptores* III.
Miller, Clement A. *Heinrich Glarean, Dodecachordon*. American Institute of Musicology, 1965.
— *Franchinus Gaffurius, Practica Musicae*. American Institute of Musicology, 1968.
Neue Deutsche Biographie, 1952- .

Niemöller, K. "Die Musica figurativa des Melchior Schanppecher", in *Beiträge zur rheinischen Musikgeschichte* 50, 1961.
— "Die Musica gregoriana des N. Wollick", in *Beiträge zur rheinischen Musikgeschichte* 11, 1955.
— "Schanppecher", in *MGG* XI.
— "Wollick", in *MGG* XIV.
Ovid. *Ars Amatoria.*
— *Fasti.*
— *Tristia.*
Pietzsch, G. "Zur Pflege der Musik an den deutschen Universitäten bis zur Mitte des 16. Jahrhunderts", in *Archiv für Musikforschung* III (1938).
Richard of St. Victor. *Excerptionum Allegoricarum Libri*, in Migne, *PL* CLXXVII.
Riemann, Hugo, ed. "Anonymi Introductorium Musicae", in *MfM* XXIX (1897), XXX (1898).
Sachs, Curt. *The History of Musical Instruments*. New York, 1940.
Schrade, Leo. "Johannes Cochlaeus, Musiktheoretiker in Köln", in *Beiträge zur rheinischen Musikgeschichte* 20, 1956.
Stäblein, Bruno, ed. "Hymnen (I)", in *Monumenta Monodica Medii Aevi.* Basel, 1956.
Strauss, G. *Nuremberg in the Sixteenth Century*. New York, 1966.
Swerdlow, Noel. "Musica dicitur a mois, quod est aqua", in *Journal of the American Musicological Society* XX, 1967.
Valla, Giorgio. "Musicae", in *De expetendis et fugiendis rebus opus*. Venice, 1501.
Vergil. *Aeneid.*
— *Ecologues.*
Virdung, Sebastian. *Musica getuscht* (1511). Facsimile ed. by L. Schrade, 1931.
Waldner, Fr. "Petrus Tritonius und das älteste gedruckte katholische Gesangbuch", in *MfM* XXVII, 1895.
Weinmann, K. *Johannes Tinctoris und sein unbekannter Traktat "De inventione et usu musicae"*. Reprint, 1961.
Wollick, N. *Opus aureum* (1501).